A Theory of Foreign Policy

PRINCETON STUDIES IN WORLD POLITICS
Number 2

PRINCETON STUDIES IN WORLD POLITICS

A Theory of Foreign Policy

GEORGE MODELSKI

Published for the Center of International Studies
Princeton University
by
FREDERICK A. PRAEGER, *Publisher*
New York

BOOKS THAT MATTER

Published in the United States of America in 1962 by
Frederick A. Praeger, Inc., Publisher
64 University Place, New York 3, N.Y.

© 1962 by Center of International Studies

Library of Congress Catalog Card Number: 62-12472

Manufactured in the United States of America

FOREWORD

Unlike theories of international relations, theories of foreign policy have been rare in recent decades. To be sure, there are emerging bodies of theory—such as organization theory, game theory, and decision-making theory—that offer useful concepts and propositions to anyone interested in studying the process of foreign-policy formation. But there have been few attempts to formulate a systematic theory of this complex process as a whole.

It was for this reason, among others, that we urged Dr. Modelski, when he was at the Center of International Studies last year, to revise his dissertation and, in the interest of economy, present its gist to a larger number of readers. We regret that this meant a deletion of bibliographical references to previous literature in this field. However, this is not a major handicap, for Dr. Modelski's approach is essentially new.

Our ability to understand and manipulate the real world depends very much on the organizing power of the concepts with which we approach reality. Relying especially on the input-output concept, Dr. Modelski's model very successfully presents and clarifies the causal processes involved in the formulation and implementation of foreign policy. His frame of reference is abstract and his propositions are general, but the explanatory power of his framework and analysis is very high.

His carefully stated propositions on the interrelation between interests and objectives, interests and power input, power input and power output, etc.—and on the adjustments between these variables, which sustain external and internal equilibrium in a foreign policy—should provide valuable tools for students and scholars concerned with the study of particular foreign policies of particular governments. Hitherto, such studies have been predominantly descriptive and historical and, lacking a clarifying structure of concepts, have obstructed comparative analysis, upon which significant additions to our knowledge of foreign-policy–making must largely rest.

KLAUS KNORR

Princeton University
July 31, 1961

PREFACE

The present monograph is the substance of a doctoral dissertation in international relations submitted to the University of London in June, 1954, under the title "A Theoretical Analysis of the Formation of Foreign Policy."*

The original argument has been preserved intact in all essentials. The difference between the dissertation and the present version is solely one of length, the wordage of the original having been nearly halved. The main body of the argument is now substantially more compact, especially in the more descriptive sections; most references to contemporary literature have been deleted. The Introduction and the Conclusion have been omitted; the former outlined the case for a theoretical approach to foreign policy, the latter discussed the methodological status of the resulting framework as a model and indicated its place in the theory of international relations. None of these points is as unfamiliar today as it was a few years ago.

A few changes have been made in terminology. The most important of these is the substitution of "input" and "output" for all textual references to "inflow" and "outflow"—the in-

* Copies may be found at the British Library of Economic and Political Science and at the University of London Library.

tention being to bring the work in closer line with the concepts of those writers who find it useful to view the political system in terms of an input-output model. I might add that at the time of writing my dissertation, input-output analysis was already current as a tool for the investigation of national economies. But my proposal to incorporate "input-output analysis of foreign policy" in the title of the proposed thesis was disallowed by a committee that included an economist, so I adopted a different title and changed the terms to "inflow-outflow." Under the circumstances, I feel free to revert to the original usage. The two other changes in terminology are the replacement of the terms "power-stock" and "power-stocking" by the more familiar "power-resources" and "power-investment."

As an exercise in clarifying the processes of foreign-policy formation—a logical-theoretical analysis of foreign policy—the work is offered here as a contribution to the emerging theory of international relations, in full awareness that foreign policy provides only one of the avenues—the study of international systems being another—along which inquiries into world politics may be pursued in a theoretical spirit.

In expressing my thanks to those who have supported me in this enterprise, I wish to give pride of place to Professor C. A. W. Manning of the London School of Economics and Political Science. In a setting none too favorable to inquiries of this kind, the work would never have been completed without his encouragement and support. I should like to thank Mr. Martin Wight for suggesting the original title for the dissertation. To Professor O. Kahn-Freund and Dr. F. S. Northedge of the University of London, to Major C. M. Kohan, and to Professor David Easton of the University of Chicago, I am indebted for reading and commenting upon the study in its original form. Professors Klaus Knorr, Harry Eckstein, and Harold Sprout of Princeton University have made valuable suggestions for bringing out this monograph.

I am grateful to the Center of International Studies and to Frederick A. Praeger for making it available to a wider audience.

GEORGE MODELSKI

The Australian National University
Canberra, A.C.T.
October 20, 1961

CONTENTS

PART ONE

THEORY OF FOREIGN POLICY

Theory and Foreign Policy

The analysis presented here expresses a position maintaining that formal deductive logic and the elaboration of analytical categories are of the utmost importance in the study of foreign policy and international relations.

Undeniably, progress in knowledge is brought about by a patient accumulation of facts and figures, and in international-relations research the empirical method has led to an emphasis on case studies and on the study of past incidents or policies. Empiricism, however, provides only a partially correct view of the way in which knowledge is advanced. Progress in scientific knowledge has always been the resultant of two interrelated developments: On the one hand, there have been significant discoveries of new facts that, by failing to fit into existing theoretical systems, have led to changes in the prevalent view of reality. On the other hand, important progress has also been achieved by the elaboration of new concepts and the development of new theories.

This view of the importance of theory construction to scientific progress is based on a number of assumptions. All reality is perceived with the help of an established set of mental constructs. Theories are elaborated systems of mental constructs of wider significance. Students of reality, including students of political reality, gain their perceptions and pursue their studies in terms of one theoretical system or another. Development of theory thus fosters the elaboration of a pre-established context of ideas in terms of which the freely accessible facts make sense.

Indeed, theory influences and furthers scientific activities in a number of ways.[1] General theory systematizes and codifies existing knowledge in the field, thus facilitating the storage and transmission of knowledge and leading to important economies in thought. Theory is a guide to research: It suggests new hypotheses to be tested, points to unresolved problems, and helps in formulating them. Theory may also exert a co-ordinating influence on the work of researchers in specialized fields. Finally, it has been pointed out that a set of verbal symbols and ideas can display some power to generate further symbols and ideas, as in mathematics, that eventually find their counterpart in the world of observable social behavior.

Theory thus serves two main purposes: It aids observation and description, and it also provides a scheme of analysis. Within a theoretical system one may, correspondingly, distinguish between a descriptive frame of reference and an analytical theory. A descriptive frame of reference may be defined as an organized system of ideas, composed of a limited number of abstract concepts whose purpose is to enable the student to select enough facts about a phenomenon to describe it adequately. Analytical theory, by contrast, explains the phenomena thus described by facilitating the construction of generalizations, permitting causal explanation of occur-

---

[1] See Talcott Parsons and Edward A. Shils, eds., *Toward a General Theory of Action* (Cambridge, Mass.: Harvard University Press, 1951), pp. 1–2; Talcott Parsons, *Essays in Sociological Theory, Pure and Applied* (Glencoe, Ill.: The Free Press, 1949), p. 18; also Barrington Moore, Jr., "The New Scholasticism and the Study of Politics," *World Politics*, VI, No. 1 (October, 1953), 130.

rences and simultaneous analysis of a body of interdependent phenomena.

In the light of this distinction, Parts II and III of this study may be said to provide a descriptive frame of reference of foreign policy, while Part IV is concerned with tracing the relations between the basic categories of the frame of reference and with generalizing about these relationships. The description of the elements of foreign-policy processes and the analysis of their interrelationships thus add up to a theory of foreign policy.

Foreign Policy as Social Action

The fact of coexistence, in the world, of a number of independent states is the starting point for all systematic study of international relations and for our analysis as well. But no matter how independent these states may be, it is an equally plain fact that the behavior of some states affects other states, either in a favorable or in an unfavorable manner. Thus, for example, the persecution of a minority in one state may arouse indignation in another state whose population may be conscious of bonds of common nationality, but it may be welcomed in a third state that experiences a similar minority problem. Or else an increase in imports may benefit the seller but disadvantage a third state because of an ensuing rise in prices, or because the increase frustrates its attempts at blockade.

This fact that the behavior of states has favorable or adverse effects on other states confronts every state with a problem: that of minimizing the adverse actions and maximizing the favorable actions of foreign states. Thus, the foreign-policy problem is essentially a question of adjusting the actions of states to each other. States deal with this problem in the same way that all the other social functions are taken care of: by entrusting some men with the special task of influencing other states. These men will henceforth be called the "policy-makers."

Naturally, the policy-makers are not the only members of a political community who devote themselves to foreign-policy problems. Tax-payers, soldiers on home or overseas duty, arms manufacturers, groups or individuals voicing claims that affect other states—all these people fill foreign-policy functions. What, then, distinguishes policy-makers from others who fill such functions? For one thing, policy-making is a full-time occupation, whereas for many of those who are not policy-makers the foreign-policy function is not the focal point of their activities. However, what particularly distinguishes policy-makers is their representative status and function, their ability to act and their responsibility for acting "on behalf" of their community. One community, and the state into which it is organized, cannot have more than one set of policy-makers who speak and act on its behalf; the availability of policy-makers is the distinguishing mark of a community organized for foreign-policy purposes, a community organized into a state.

Policy-makers are an essential component of the process of making foreign policy. In the absence of representatives, no organized relations between states could be carried on. Policy-makers fill the crucial role of representative agents (not principals), of intermediaries or go-betweens. Although they are not neutral intermediaries, because their primary loyalties belong to their community, they constitute an essential instrument whose function is mediation between that community and the outside world.

The influence of the community on the making of policy has been likened to the role played by buyers in a commodity market. "The public share in policy decisions may be compared, with important qualifications, to a market. It buys or refuses to buy the 'policy products' offered by competing elites."[2] This metaphor describes only one segment of policy formation: the relations between the community and the policy-makers. To present a complete view of the policy-making process, the picture of the sale of policy products to the public should be supplemented by a picture of the processes whereby policy-makers "manufacture" these products. Policy-making involves considerations of supply (production), as well as those of demand (consumption).

A close comparison can be drawn between the functions of policy-makers and those of lawyers. Lawyers are instructed by, and act on behalf of, their clients. Their job is to attempt, through negotiation or litigation, to change the behavior of other people in a direction favorable to the interests of their clients, or to advise their clients of the impossibility of doing so. Without pushing this comparison too far, we may say that it brings out at least one point: that the lawyer, like the policy-maker, deals with two distinct sets of people—with his clientele (his community), who instruct him and supply the resources with which to carry out his functions, and with the outside world, whose behavior he engages in efforts to change.

We may now call the stream (or flow) of actions coming from the community and directed toward the policy-maker his "input," and the actions toward the outside world in which the policy-maker himself engages on his community's behalf his "output." Policy-makers can thus be pictured as occupying that crucial point at which inputs are transformed into outputs; it is this key position that accounts for their importance to foreign-policy analysis: Inputs and outputs can be defined only by reference to policy-makers.

Although it may be true to say that there is no single locus of foreign-policy decision-making—decisions that affect foreign policy are made all the time, at all levels, inside and out-

[2] Gabriel A. Almond, *The American People and Foreign Policy* (New York: Frederick A. Praeger, 1960), p. 6.

side the government—foreign policy has, and must have, a focus both for practical and for theoretical reasons. In practice, the policy-making power must be traceable to a limited number of individuals in supreme authority who, because of their supreme authority, are able to determine the over-all direction of policy, who can coordinate the activities of subordinate agencies and iron out disagreements between them, who can overrule lower-level decisions that are contrary to general policy, and who do, in fact, assume responsibility for what happens, so that they can be blamed for failure and praised for success. We know, furthermore, that in every state an experienced observer can identify those few individuals who are responsible for the making of foreign policy in that state. We may add that the concept of policy-makers as the focus of foreign-policy–making is indispensable on theoretical grounds because it serves as the reference point for the entire analysis. Since all the other foreign-policy activities stand in some relation to policy-makers, and since policy-makers can be conceived of as standing midway between inputs and outputs, their activities are a natural focus for the analysis of foreign policy. The focal concept of "policy-makers" introduces order into the confused welter of forces and influences that make up foreign policy; it must therefore be retained.

We may point out at this stage that the stream of actions flowing from the community to the policy-makers is a one-way process. Since the policy-maker is conceived of as an agent of the community, his activities in relation to his community are not held to have independent significance of their own, but are governed by the duties of his office and the exigencies imposed by the behavior of other states. That is why attention is focused on the actions of the community rather than on the actions of the policy-maker in relation to his community.

Foreign policy is the system of activities evolved by communities for changing the behavior of other states and for adjusting their own activities to the international environment. Within it, two types of activities may be singled out for special attention: the inputs flowing into it, and the output it produces. The foremost task of foreign-policy analysis must be to throw light on the ways in which states attempt to change, and succeed in changing, the behavior of other states.

The element of "action" is prominent in most conceptions of foreign policy, and in this study, too, foreign policy is looked upon as a system of social action. Definitions also speak of policy as a "course," *une ligne*, implying that this action must be consistent and rational, as indeed it must be. This element of consistency associated with rationality and reflection has been emphasized in other definitions that conceive of foreign policy as a system of ideas referring to future action, as a plan or program of action, rather than as action itself. But the planning or programming of policies is as much a type of action as the execution of policies. While on occasion it may be useful to distinguish between "policy as planned" (*ex ante*) and "policy as executed" (*ex post*)—in reality two standpoints from which one and the same policy, or action, may be contemplated—it does not seem necessary to incorporate this distinction between the plan of action and the action itself into our basic definition.

The concept of "action" is not a newcomer to the social sciences. On several occasions it has served as the starting point for sociological inquiries. Max Weber's *Wirtschaft und Gesellschaft*, for instance, begins with a definition of social action. The burden of Professor Talcott Parsons' first treatise was to show that essentially the same type of theory—namely, what he calls the "voluntaristic theory of action"—had appeared in the works of a number of earlier social scientists.

In *The Structure of Social Action*, Parsons drew attention to the fact that scientific inquiry tends to isolate phenomena and then proceeds to break them into units or parts. For him, the basic unit of the theory of action is the "unit act," defined in terms of certain basic, descriptive properties:

(1) It implies an agent, an "actor." (2) For purposes of definition the act must have an "end," a future state of affairs toward which the process of action is oriented. (3) It must be initiated in a "situation" of which the trends of development differ in one or more important respects from the state of affairs to which the action is oriented, the end. This situation is in turn analyzable into two elements: those over which the actor has no control, that is which he cannot alter, or prevent from being altered, in conformity with his end, and those over which he has such control. The former may be termed the "conditions" of action, the latter the "means." Finally (4) there is inherent in the conception of this unit . . . a certain mode of relationship between these elements. That is, in the choice of alternative means to the end, in so far as the situation allows alternatives, there is a "normative orientation" of action.[3]

Such are the elements of the unit act. Parsons discusses the implications of the unit act, the relation between these elements and between unit acts, and the problems of order and rationality arising out of these relations. His analysis of social action is prominently based on two conceptual schemes of long standing in Western thought: the distinction between ends and means, and the organism-environment (situation) dichotomy. Indeed, Parsons' motto for his treatise, which, incidentally, could serve as well as the motto for the present study, is a quotation from one of Weber's methodological essays: "*Jede denkende Besinnung auf die letzten Elemente sinnvollen menschlichen Handelns is zunächst gebunden an die Kategorien 'Zweck' und 'Mittel.'* "[4] Ends and means are the cornerstones of all theorizing about human action, and they must also be incorporated into the theory of foreign policy.

[3] Talcott Parsons, *The Structure of Social Action* (New York: McGraw-Hill Book Company, 1937), p. 44.
[4] "All serious reflection about the ultimate elements of human conduct is oriented primarily in terms of the categories 'end' and 'means.' " From *Max Weber on the Methodology of the Social Sciences*, tr. and ed. by Edward A. Shils and Henry A. Finch (Glencoe, Ill.: The Free Press, 1949), p. 52.

We shall now outline the elements of foreign policy that emerge as the result of combining the input-output concepts with the elementary properties of the unit act, and in particular the ends-means schema. In other words, the actions that in this study go by the name of "inputs" and "outputs" will, like the unit act, be defined as possessing ends and means as well as the other properties of the unit act. The "elements of foreign policy" or "policy elements" thus devised are, of course, no more than categories of description, mental constructs in terms of which influences bearing upon foreign policy are classified.

Assuming that foreign policy is a system of action, who are the "actors" in this game? We have already noted the crucial role of policy-makers. They define the interests of the community, formulate the objectives of foreign policy, and are in control of the state's power. Theirs is a key role: They are the unifying and regulating element for all segments of political action, the sensitive control mechanisms at the heart of foreign policy. Nonetheless, policy-makers are not the only actors in the drama of foreign policy; all those members of the community whose actions (inputs) are relevant to foreign policy must also be considered as actors within the foreign-policy frame of reference.

Furthermore, we assume that all these actions can be conceived of as having an "end"; that they tend to bring about a future state of affairs, defined as the desirable behavior of other states, that would not prevail had the action not taken place. Future desirable behavior of other states is, of course, the only future state of affairs (ends) with which foreign-policy analysis is concerned. States of affairs that cannot be changed by influencing other states' foreign policies—or in which change is not considered desirable—do not come within the scope of foreign-policy analysis. The future desirable behavior of other states is defined as the "aims" of foreign policy, and in accordance with the distinction between inputs and outputs we differentiate between *interests* and *objectives*, the interests being the aims conveyed to the policy-makers by members of the community, and the objectives the conceptions of future desirable behavior of other states implicit in the policy-makers' actions in relations with the outside world. We can subsume both interests and objectives under the heading of "aims," because this future desirable behavior of other states is the aim both of the policy-makers in their dealings with the outside world and of the community in its relations with the policy-makers.

Actions also stand in a certain relation with, or are oriented toward, a number of norms or principles. Every such principle is a command to act in a certain way by virtue of a sentiment that such an action is worth doing for its own sake. The sentiments that certain foreign-policy activities are desirable in themselves may be termed the "principles" of foreign policy.

Action involves the application of means. The policy-makers may be thought of as being in command of certain instruments whose use tends to bring about the desired future behavior of other states. These instruments, viewed analytically, are that part of the situation, human and nonhuman, that the policy-makers are in a position to control. In international relations, it is becoming customary (although there is no complete agreement on this point) to use the word "power" for the totality of means that a state can draw on in the pursuit of foreign policy. We shall henceforth use "power" in the sense of being the "means" of foreign policy; and in accordance with the distinction between input and output, we shall differentiate between *power-input*, the services and resources put at the disposal of the policy-makers by the community for foreign-policy purposes, and *power-output*, the expenditure of power in foreign-policy operations toward the outside world.

We must also mention the context of foreign policy, the situation within which every foreign policy operates. The significant environment of every foreign policy, in so far as it cannot be regarded as "power" of that policy, is the foreign policies of other states, including those states whose behavior (policies) is to be changed. Apart from policies of members of the international society, there are no other facts that are relevant or significant to the analysis of foreign policy. The only significant facts are those that are reflected in foreign policies.

To summarize, the basic concepts of our theory of foreign policy, obtained as the result of the combination of the elementary properties of the "unit act" with the concepts of input and output, are as follows: (1) policy-makers; (2) aims of foreign policy, including interests and objectives; (3) principles of foreign policy; (4) power, including power-input and power-output; and (5) context of foreign policy. It is with the help of these concepts that the task of describing and analyzing foreign policy will be attempted.

Decision-making and the Tasks of Policy-makers

The view that foreign policy consists of the making of decisions is well on the way to becoming part of conventional wisdom, but the problem of decision-making is hardly a new one to students of human behavior. There are a number of advantages attached to the use of the concept of "decision" in the analysis of foreign policy. This tool of thought is based on the insight that a chosen course of action is only one of several alternatives and that the choice should be guided by ends and means. As a device for the analysis of action it proceeds from the truism that every action begins with a decision, and it explains actions in terms of the decisions that originated them. There is little value in objecting that in real life, or even in international life, actions or policies do not always, or even in the majority of cases, begin with a decision. "Decision-making" is an "ideal type" in Weber's sense, a mental construct rather than an account of reality. This mental construct makes it possible for the observer to interpret and criticize actions as if they had been preceded by a decision. Furthermore, it allows him to make a more authoritative guess about the kind of decision that preceded any particular action. Decision-making need not be a description of actual decisions, but it does suggest how decisions should, ideally, be arrived at. It promotes rationality in action and rationality in foreign policy.

Such considerations suggest that there is considerable attraction and plausibility in conceiving of international relations, and even more of foreign policy, in terms of decision-making. The decision provides a peg on which much of the pertinent information can be hung, and it also serves as a stimulant toward further research. But granted that it is a possible way of organizing knowledge about foreign policy, is it the most propitious way of doing so? There appear to be important reasons against considering foreign policy, and also international relations, predominantly in terms of decision-making.

First of all, objection must be raised against the more extreme statement that "the activities of statesmen, in fact, all foreign affairs, can be reduced to the making of specific decisions." This conveys a picture of the policy-making process that, if not incorrect, is too restrictive and theoretically unsatisfactory.

The picture of policy-making created by such a statement is that of an important person, sitting in his office and receiving callers and assistants, each of whom presents an issue upon which a decision is required. After reflection, the important person presumably arrives at the "big decision." Although containing an element of truth, this is a warped picture of the activities of statesmen. All human actions, it may be said, can be reduced to the making of decisions; and yet a statement like that does not carry us very far toward understanding human behavior. All human beings have to make decisions;

statesmen are not alone in this respect. Thus, the activities of statesmen cannot be defined solely in terms of decision-making. One must describe in more detail the type of problem, the type of decision, with which statesmen are called upon to deal. Their specific activities are determined by the sort of functions they are required to perform, and therefore the concept of the tasks and duties of policy-makers gives a more correct view of their activities, and of the responsibilities arising from their unique position as intermediaries between their community and the international society, than the concept of "decision-making."

Moreover, often conceived of as a succession of separate responses to world events, "decision-making" tends to ignore the continuous stream of activities within which decisions are embedded, and pays little heed, in theory at least, to the actions that link one decision to another. A workable conception of foreign policy should put greater emphasis on the continuity of all foreign-policy processes; it should be supplemented by emphasis on foresight, on the necessity for constant preoccupation with the future, on what might perhaps be called "strategic planning."

Pervading the approach through decision-making is the suggestion that the innermost skill required for the conduct of foreign policy is the capacity to think clearly and solve complex problems correctly. Yet policy-making cannot be reduced to decision-making on the basis of a flow of information handled in an "administrative" fashion. The activities of policy-makers—and foreign policy does not consist only of the activities of policy-makers—are defined by a number of functions, each of which requires, in addition to the capacity to make decisions and to think clearly, such other skills as an ability to handle men and win the confidence of groups, to voice and mold interests, to organize foreign-policy operations, and to exercise foresight.

Undue emphasis on decision-making leads to a "genetic

fallacy," for it implies that an account of the origins of a policy—that is, of the decision initiating that policy—adequately explains the entire policy. But the study of a foreign-policy decision can reveal only a part of what may be known about a policy and of what it is important to know. There is more to a policy than the decision that initiated it.

Finally, the concept of decision-making provides a tool for explaining some of the grand occasions of foreign policy, such as the decisions to enter a war, to embark on an assistance program, or to initiate some other major policies. It is less handy for explaining a great number of perhaps less weighty, but nonetheless significant, actions. Thus negotiations or international conferences do not fit easily into the scheme; such common activities of statesmen as speech-making, press conferences, public statements, travels at home and abroad, and the dispatch of diplomatic notes cannot be easily accommodated within the framework of decision-making. Furthermore, the decision-making conception fails to bring the actions of the community sufficiently into the picture of the foreign-policy process, conveying the implication that these actions, the interests they express, and the power-input they provide are merely incidental to the process of foreign policy. Since foreign policy cannot be reduced to the activities of policy-makers, it cannot, *a fortiori*, be limited to the making of decisions by policy-makers.

These considerations suggest that the idea of policy as a succession of decisions is in itself inadequate as the central organizing concept for the study of foreign policy. We may retain the concept of "decision" for the analysis of the inception of an operation; we cannot dispense with the concept of alternative policies between which a choice must be made. But we shall pay much more attention to the entire web of activities in which the decision is merely one incident, and center attention on the tasks of policy-makers as the locus of political action.

The policy-makers have previously been conceived of as situated midway between inputs and outputs. This central position in relation to the foreign-policy process imposes on them special tasks in relation to all of the four elements of foreign policy. These are tasks every policy-maker performs, no matter what foreign policy a country is pursuing. They are a necessary part of all foreign policy. They may be performed efficiently or inefficiently, but they must always be performed in some manner.

The policy-makers' tasks and the activities to which they give rise may be classified conveniently and systematically by reference to the four elements that constitute the foreign-policy process. Every policy-maker must concern himself with (1) the formulation of interests, (2) the procurement of power-input, (3) the definition of objectives, and (4) the allocation of power-output. The acquisition of information on which to base policy and the handing out of information about policy are other tasks related to each of these four elements.

The acquisition of information pertinent to foreign policy has always been regarded as one of the important fields of action for the policy-maker. The modern statesman has at his disposal an intricate apparatus for supplying him with information about developments relating to his own foreign policy and with intelligence about the foreign policy of other states. The policy-maker's first task in this field is to guide information-gathering activities into purposeful channels by asking the right questions, posing the right problems, and communicating the purposes for which information is to be gathered. Policy-makers must also ensure that the intelligence effort runs smoothly, and to this end they must set up intelligence collection agencies if none exist, and support the existing agencies by supplying them with sufficient resources. The interpretation of collected information, the conversion of facts into knowledge, is also a top policy-making job and cannot be delegated to subordinates. Finally, results of intelligence efforts must be incorporated into policy.

The policy-maker needs information about the four main elements of his state's foreign policy and about the foreign policy of other states. In the field of interests, his primary duty is to ascertain the wishes and desires of his community. Most often the difficulty lies not so much in keeping aware of the general wishes of the community as in maintaining contact with all the interests involved in a variety of current issues. The importance of being correctly informed about power-input can hardly be exaggerated. Many a disaster has resulted from the overvaluation of one's power. Power-input is not a constant quantity; it changes all the time and the policy-maker cannot but try to keep abreast of these changes. The collection of information in the fields of objectives and power-output is essentially a problem of finding out how the organizations engaged in the execution of foreign policy are acquitting themselves of their tasks. Reporting and control devices must be instituted to keep the policy-maker in contact with developments in this sphere of responsibility, which is peculiarly his own. Lastly, the most obvious segment of the intelligence effort is the collection of information about the foreign policies of other states. The assessment of these policies, in respect to both aims and power, is very closely connected with the determination of a state's foreign policy.

A broadly conceived and carefully executed intelligence effort is the foundation of sound policy-making. But policy-makers have other specific tasks to perform in relation to each of the four elements of foreign policy. In the field of interests, the tasks of policy-makers are not confined to the passive ascertainment of the demands and wishes of their community. Such requests may be incoherent or fragmentary, they may conflict with accepted interests, and their full implications may be uncertain. Policy-makers do not accept every request that is put to them; they urge caution on some members of their community, and impress others with the advantages of a compromise. They thus play an active part in the formulation of what are held to be the country's interests: They are the true brokers in interests.

Policy-makers also act as the interpreters of the interests of foreign countries to their own community. The interests of other countries, and in particular those of friendly powers, need to be explained to the community because they are often far from self-evident. Policy-makers are not alone in championing the claims of allies before the internal community. Strong sections of opinion frequently take up the cause of friendly powers and adopt it as part of their own demands in the field of foreign policy. As a rule, however, the policy-maker is the person best placed to serve as the day-to-day interpreter of the interests of other countries, both within the government, to government departments and public authorities, and outside it, to the public at large. He may be able to take a more charitable view of actions of friendly powers that threaten the interests of some section of his community.

In the field of power-input, the policy-maker's task is to ensure that the community allocates to foreign-policy purposes such amounts of power-input (services and resources) as are adequate to safeguard and implement the interests that have been formulated. This is perhaps the most thankless of his tasks, for it amounts to inducing people to make what are sometimes considerable sacrifices. On coming into office, nearly every government, except that of a newly founded state, inherits a more or less going concern, a habitual minimum of power-input. The inhabitants pay taxes, join the armed forces, and generally serve the state almost as a matter of course, and it takes considerable provocation and oppression of important sections of the community for these habitual services to be withheld. More difficult is the task of the policy-maker who wishes to enlarge his power-input. Such enlargement necessitates changes in the behavior of numbers of people, both

within and outside the country, some of whom must be induced to transfer their services to foreign-policy purposes (for
instance, through conscription), while others must acquiesce
in going without services they previously received (perhaps because of higher taxes). Such changes are invariably painful.
Yet a policy-maker's stature is never better displayed than at
times of great crisis when he appeals to his community for
major sacrifices. The preparation and organization of internal
and international support for foreign policy are among the
great tasks of policy-makers.

The third specific task of policy-makers relates to the definition of objectives. But if they are to be made explicit and,
above all, communicated to others, they must emerge as the
product of solitary cogitation, intimate discussion, and wider
deliberation. Some of them, such as those associated with national defense, may be obvious or traditional. The policy-
makers' special task is to meet with an appropriate definition
of objectives any new situation as it arises on the international
scene or results from changes in the other elements of foreign
policy. Objectives are defined by means of the reflections of
individual policy-makers, and perhaps to an even greater extent through private discussions in policy-making committees
such as a cabinet, a council of ministers, a political bureau,
and the like. Individual proposals or working papers can be
put forward in such committees and then amended in the
light of criticism. The effect of criticism is to coordinate the
new objective with existing programs of action. Definition of
objectives implies not only the laying down of isolated plans
of action, but also the coordination of diverse actions, not
necessarily into a "master plan," but certainly into an internally consistent policy.

Once these objectives have been defined, they must be
communicated to those who are to execute them. The in-
jection of a sense of purpose into an organization cannot
result from formal instructions alone; private letters or inter-

views, confidential background papers, speeches to group leaders and other selected audiences, all help to convey a sense of mission to those on whose ready response to leadership depends the success of policy. Objectives must also be brought to the notice of other states. Policy-makers may manifest their objectives by announcing their country's concern about a problem, or writing notes of protest in which they specify the behavior they expect of other states, or stating their country's attitude at international conferences. Finally, policy-makers must see to it that the objectives are in fact implemented. This implies in part the task of preventing any action that does not conform to the original definition of objectives, and it also implies the taking of positive action wherever the execution of policy meets with an obstacle. These are control tasks accomplished through the supervision of the executors of policy, the study of reports, visits and inspection tours, and representations with other states. The devising of proper controls for gauging the performance of the organizations executing foreign policy is in itself a major policy-making function.

The fourth group of the policy-makers' tasks arises in connection with power-output and the allocation of power to foreign-policy operations. Above all, the allocation of power-output entails operational decisions: decisions to start, change, or break off actions aimed at altering the foreign policy of other states. These are decisions to commit the government's resources to foreign-policy purposes. They crystallize in orders and directives to those who execute government policy, and in negotiations and consultations to bring about the commitment of other states. The task of allocating power-output includes responsibility for the redistribution of resources among policies in accordance with changing requirements and for the distribution of power-output as among present uses, future uses, and the service of liabilities. Lastly, the policy-maker must be concerned with the efficiency with which policy is executed; his aim must be to produce the maximum results with the least outlay of power-output.

The final point to be mentioned in connection with these tasks is the obverse of the duty of collecting information with which this discussion started; it is the task of putting out information about policy, the necessity for policy-makers to explain and justify their policies. Policy-makers are agents who act on behalf of their community; they are therefore expected to report periodically upon the performance of their functions.

Having concluded the discussion of the tasks of policy-makers that are the necessary features of foreign policy, let us now turn to a detailed account of the four "variable" elements involved in foreign policy: power-input, power-output, interests, and objectives.

PART TWO

ON POWER

A student of foreign policy needs little, if any, excuse for laying emphasis upon power; the concept bulks large in the literature of international relations. Yet it cannot be readily said that the theorizing in this branch of foreign-policy analysis is of the highest quality. At present, the study of power has become associated with the proposition that "Power is the generalized end of all politics," but the detailed treatment of the subject has been strongly descriptive and lacking in analytical penetration. The concept of power has been divorced from problems of action and, as of now, is scarcely relevant to foreign-policy analysis.

Our own interest in power is limited to the power that states exert upon each other in the business of looking after their interests. Hobbes defined "the power of a man" as "his present means to obtain some future apparent good." For purposes of foreign-policy analysis, we shall define power as the community's present means to obtain the future desirable behavior of other states.

In this context, a distinction can be drawn between *governmental power* and *national power*. Governmental power may be defined as the means that are put at the policy-makers' disposal by the community and that they currently employ in actions aimed at altering the foreign policies of other states.

Conceptually at least, this is a fairly determinate quantity: It is the part of the resources of a community that is devoted to foreign-policy purposes under the control of the government, and it is this power that is the object of our analysis.

The quantity that might be called "national power" is more difficult to indicate with certainty. At any one moment, the government does not have at its disposal all the power it could possibly have; rather, governmental power is the power that the government has succeeded in obtaining from the community for foreign-policy aims and that the community has consented to devote to those aims. There are occasions, such as wars for national survival—which are waged bitterly and without "cost accounting"—when governmental power coincides with national power, when the total effort exerted is the maximum that could possibly be exerted. But such efforts are rare; on most occasions, governmental power is well below the maximum attainable, and it will tend toward an optimum that is reached after foreign-policy aims have been reconciled with other purposes of national action.

We need "national power" as a limiting concept, a concept indicating the magnitude of effort that a community can bring itself to produce in the gravest of emergencies. National power is not liable to sudden changes, in contrast to governmental power, which tends to fluctuate in accordance with the urgency of devoting resources to national policy. National-power estimates figure, for instance, in comparisons of the capacities of two states for sustained war, whereas in all estimates of immediate reactions it is governmental power that is at stake. Power estimates also usually focus attention on means that are positively and actually at the government's or the community's disposal. They do not point directly to the weak points, the tender spots of a government; such vulnerabilities are revealed by implication alone, by the fact that power is not available. A study of the divergencies between governmental and national power reveals such weak points and suggests ways in which they may be prevented or exploited.

We must now fit the concept of power into the wider canvas of international life. Power is commonly recognized as a social phenomenon; it is constantly created as the product of social relationships. We have recognized power as the state's present means, as its ability to act on the international scene. The ability to act is basically and essentially affected by the degree to which men can be induced to further foreign-policy objectives. Why do men act as policy-makers wish them to? Because their own purposes are being satisfied in the process, either concurrently with these actions, or because of considerations they have received in the past or expect to receive in the future. Power is the product of cooperation between the policy-makers and their community.

Components of Power-input

The foreign-policy problem is with us all the time. Thus the processes whereby the community supplies its policy-makers with services and resources to enable them to deal with this problem, and the processes by which that power is expended in efforts to deal with it, must be continuous, too. They can be conceived of as continuous streams of action over time. (Power is only an aspect, or "element," of action, but there can be no power without action.) However, these streams of action never remain constant; they fluctuate all the time. Policy-makers may be annoyed if the substantial measure of support they have been enjoying one year dwindles away to very little the next year, but they should never claim to be surprised. Power-inputs and power-outputs thus are "variable" elements of foreign policy. It is these variations in the power of a state, their cause and their effects, rather than the absolute degree of power, that deserve the most emphasis in our study.

The power-input–power-output distinction is analogous to the economists' concepts of income and expenditure. Power-input could be said to be the income that policy-makers receive from their community for policy purposes; power-output, the spending of this income on foreign-policy operations. But the concepts of power-input and power-output are wider in scope and serve different purposes than the concepts of the economists. Income and expenditure connote money and the services that money can buy; power includes aspects of action that are not subject to economic exchange and that are outside the market process.

What are the principal components of power-input?

The first criterion of power-input is the source from which it is derived. Roughly, power-input can be said to come either from within the state or from other states, and accordingly it is possible to talk of the *internal* and *external* power-inputs of a state. Such a differentiation is convenient because it indicates that, in the case of power-input derived from internal sources, the government is dealing mostly with "municipal" organizations and with its own nationals, whereas in the case of external power-input it is dependent on the actions of other states. There are significant differences in the probabilities of behavior of groups within and outside the state. The government can hope to exercise greater control over internal than over external power-input. On the other hand, internal power-input must be organized and directed by the government; external power-input comes to hand ready-made, as it were, and the recipient state reaps the fruits of another government's organizing efforts.

In one way, all power is the ability of organizations to attain the aims set for them. Yet, for theoretical purposes, such ability must be understood to comprise not only the services of the personnel making up these organizations, but also the services of goods, supplies, and other material resources without which organizations cannot function. The goods and services necessary to the functioning of organizations may be called the "nonhuman" elements of power, as distinct from the "human" components of power, which are the services of personnel. Power-input must, furthermore, be understood to consist not only of the current services of organizational personnel (and the current receipts of goods and matériel) but also of the advantageous results (that is, services) of past and future actions. The results of past actions that yield present services, and will continue doing so, are defined as "power-resources." (Analogous to the economists' concepts of "capital" and "wealth," they might also be called foreign-policy resources or assets.) The present benefit from projected future actions may be called the "value of promises."

An illustration of these distinctions may be appropriate at this point. A fortress—Gibraltar, for instance—is a good example of a power-resource. Its existence is due to past exertions of British foreign policy. At any given time, the control of this fortress affords the British government certain services, such as the ability to control the traffic between the Atlantic and the Mediterranean, and thereby to influence to some extent the policies of states dependent on this traffic. In the fortress, there may also be in existence at any time stores of goods, such as oil in storage tanks or stocks of food and ammunition. These stores are power-resources because they result from past accumulation and because their existence yields considerable benefits—for instance, insurance against sudden attack or other emergencies. The services of this fortress, and also the services of the goods stores, must be reckoned in a computation of power-input as the services of power-resources. But it should be pointed out that it is the *services* of power-assets, the current advantages of having a fortress or reserves, that are being computed, and not the power-resource itself, not the value of the fortress or of the reserves as such. The power-resources of a state deserve a separate reckoning.

In keeping with these distinctions, we recognize three types of power-input: (1) the services of power-resources (the present results of past resource-accumulation); (2) currently compensated personnel services and matériel supplies (i.e., those not attributable to past accumulation); (3) the value of promises (the present benefits of incurring a future liability). Each of these power-inputs may be either internal or external and may have both human and nonhuman components. Finally, a residual component of power-input is the value of the services of the policy-makers themselves, and also that part of power-input rendered to policy-makers on the basis not of current, past, or future advantage, but of the understanding and the claim that they best promote the general interests of the community.

Foremost among the components of human internal power-input are the current services of those governmental organizations whose direct function is to influence the conduct of foreign states. From now on these will be called the "foreign-policy organizations." They comprise the diplomatic service, including the staffs of the foreign ministry and members of the consular service; the armed forces, with their supply and intelligence organizations; the communication services and other officials who deal primarily with actions affecting other states, such as members of information and propaganda services and those handling trade and financial relations; and staffs assisting the policy-makers, including the heads of government. The services of all these are provided on a full-time basis, and to them must be added the nonvoluntary services of military and other conscripts who make up a large proportion of national military manpower.

The citizens at large, on the other hand, do not put themselves directly at the service of foreign policy. It is neither desirable nor necessary that they should do so; social division of labor requires that only a certain proportion of the population, and a small one at that, devote itself to the conduct and execution of foreign policy. (In times of crisis, however, a much greater proportion may be called upon to do so.) If the majority of the citizens worked for foreign-policy objectives, there would be little time and opportunity for them to attend to the many other purposes that a complex society pursues all the time. Payment of taxes in their various forms, subscriptions to state loans, and various kinds of voluntary part-time work are some of the ways in which citizens put a part of their efforts and time at the disposal of the government for the purposes of foreign policy. The citizens' contributions are utilized in two principal ways: A portion serves to recompense and reward those directly engaged in foreign-policy operations and so enables them to claim a share of the national product; another portion provides the government and its foreign-policy organizations with those nonhuman resources that it needs for the conduct of its business.

Another part of a government's internal power-input is the services of internal power-resources. Let us first consider the services of the human components of these resources. The services of power-resources, it may be recalled, are those that are due to past acts of foreign policy (to past power-output). In their human aspects, as far as they relate to organizational personnel, power-resources comprise all those qualities of human organization and national action that are indispensable ingredients of successful foreign policy but that cannot be created overnight. These include, among others, the smooth efficiency of a long-established diplomatic service, the morale of an army with battle honors to its credit, the technical know-how and social experience of every citizen-soldier, the expertise of officialdom, the established channels of communication and, finally, the moral cohesion of a united nation. Analytically, the services of human power-resources may not be easy to separate from those resulting from current exertions; they are nonetheless real and can be summed up under the heading of the "benefits of training and experience," benefits that are universally acknowledged and that nations attempt to obtain by subjecting young human beings to prolonged training before they become full members of society. The importance of human power-resources lies in the fact that the formation, or the changing, of any distinct pattern of human behavior is a process that requires time and energy; the ready availability of the services of experienced human organizations is therefore an undeniable advantage to every policy-maker.

Two main types of power-resources may be distinguished: power-resources in current use, and reserves. The preceding paragraph indicated the part played by human power-resources in current use. There remains to be pointed out the importance of reserves. They not only are a significant component of power-input, because their availability is a necessary precondition for the smooth running of all organizations, but they assume crucial importance when the scale of foreign-policy operations is suddenly expanded. If it is to be successful, such an expansion—e.g., the mobilization of an army—can be effected only by drawing upon accumulated reserves, human and nonhuman (for instance, stockpiles of raw materials). In the field of human reserves we have to deal, above all, with the reserves of the armed forces, with plans and preparations (not only of a military kind) that have been drawn up for future emergencies, with that total pool of trained and adaptable manpower that a government can draw upon to fill vacant posts and to enlarge the national effort in any direction. In certain situations, individual citizens—and, in times of stress, large numbers of them—may offer the government an extra increment of service over and above their usual services. A successful government may reckon upon such good will on the part of its citizens as part of its reserves. Population figures set an upper limit to the human power-resources of the government; they are the measure of national power. But in many circumstances governmental power will be significantly smaller.

The nonhuman components of internal power-resources have traditionally received more adequate treatment in discussions of the "elements of national power." There is indeed little difficulty in identifying the national territory as the most important component of nonhuman power-resources. The size of that territory provides the upper limit rather than an exact indication of the magnitude of national resources. Control over territory supplies the government with many irreplaceable services. First of all, territory is the necessary condition of the existence of a state. Governmental organizations can exist only in a space that is not occupied by any other governmental organizations. Furthermore, territory provides the foundation on which all the remaining governmental and national internal resources are situated. The loss of part of the territory entails the loss of proportionate amounts of other power-resources. Finally, control over a territory confers on the government advantages that no other government can obtain from that territory at the same time: the ability freely to move men and matériel, a claim to that territory's natural resources and to the air space above it, and an opportunity to exert pressure on the nearby territories of other states. The possession of strategically placed territory lends mobility to foreign policy.

On the territory are to be found the main elements of a state's internal resources. Three groups of nonhuman resources can, in the main, be distinguished: (1) the equipment, the permanent instllations, and the matériel reserves (including, e.g., atomic-weapon stockpiles) of the armed forces; (2) the transport and communication systems, which in most countries are under government control; and (3) that part of the country's industrial equipment facilities that serves and supplies the government. Little need be added in explanation of these three categories of power-resources; they provide services that are essential to the execution of the foreign policy of every state. They are discussed at length in textbooks and monographs, together with territory and population. We may merely add that the subject of industrial equipment pro-

vides a particularly significant instance of the distinction between governmental and national power. Few governments,
and then only on rare occasions, can obtain the services of the
entire industrial complex of their states for foreign-policy purposes. But a large part of the industrial equipment is rightly
regarded as reserve capacity.

One more dimension of internal power-input remains to be
considered: that which is received on the strength of future
services. Just as services of power-resources represent a return
for past exertions, parts of current power-input may be received in anticipation of future actions or, better still, on the
strength of promises to perform certain future actions. In
this sense it is possible to speak of power-input as being due
to "promises," implied or explicit. An important instance of
internal power-input thus derived is loans made by the citizens
to the state. One can also say that most relationships contain
an element of reference to future services, for the simple
reason that an exact return for services obtained cannot
always be given conveniently at the time of the services. To
some extent, loyalty to policy-makers may be said to be an
instance in which power-input is based on the expectation of
future, not immediate, returns. At this point, a distinction
might be drawn between the availability of services based on
promises—that is, the presence of a willingness to render
services now in return for some future reward—and the services received against a promise. The former is an asset, part of
the power-resources of a state—in any case in so far as this
confidence has been inspired by past actions. The trust placed
by citizens in their government is an important foreign-policy
resource; if promises are to be believed, they must be based on
trust, which is the result of past record. But confidence is only
part of the decision to exchange present for future services:
Among other relevant considerations is the amount of the
reward to be obtained, and for this reason services based on
promises require separate treatment.

Let us now turn to the subject of external power-inputs. External power-inputs, it will be recalled, are those components of power-input that are derived from outside the state and are the consequence of actions of other states. This subject has not so far received the attention it deserves; it is scarcely mentioned in the textbooks or among the orthodox "elements of national power." A powerful state needs not only devoted servants in its foreign-policy organizations, but also friends and allies. "Therefore," said Hobbes, "to have servants is Power, to have friends is Power: for they are strengths united."

A nation without friends counts for little in the society of states. Alliances and friendships are the basis of the influence a state exercises in international society. The external power-input obtained within the framework of these friendships and alliances requires a treatment separate from that accorded to internal power-input, because the techniques required to create them are different. In the one case, policy-makers deal with members of their own state, whereas in the case of external power-inputs they negotiate with other states. Although from the point of view of power-input the two cases are of equal importance, the ebb and flow of external power-input are much more the substance of international relations. They are the *quid pro quo* of international exchanges, the essence of most diplomatic history, and, par excellence, the subject matter of diplomacy.

Foremost among the components of the external power-input are those actions that other states perform in exchange, or in compensation, for services currently received. The following are the most important groups of services thus to be obtained:

1. Supporting actions taken toward third states. These are commonly referred to as "diplomatic support," but their range is wide and covers a variety of enterprises, such as expressions of concern—for instance, at press conferences or in speeches—at a third state's actions; diplomatic representa-

tions to third states; support for foreign-policy positions and proposals at international conferences and in voting—e.g., in the U.N. General Assembly; declarations of support in moments of crisis, including announcements of willingness to fight a common war; and, finally, such important steps as actual entry into a common struggle. Such support is highly valuable to any state, but it is also difficult to control. It is valuable because the actions of policy-makers of other states, whatever the degree of commitment, are backed by the entire power of these states; it is as if a state's power were doubled or trebled, according to the amount of support received on an issue. On the other hand, this type of support is susceptible to little control: It must be requested through diplomatic channels; its execution and its form are within the other state's discretion; it is always liable to be discontinued. That is why dependability is a quality much looked for in an alliance partner.

2. Actions of other states' organizations lending direct assistance to the foreign-policy organization. This type of support ranges wide, too; it covers exchanges of small services and day-to-day cooperation between two friendly governments and may include the cooperation, including coordination of actions, of the diplomatic representatives of two states in the capital of a third, exchanges of information between the intelligence services of two countries, exchanges of view and comparisons of plans by military staffs, and consultations preceding new policy decisions. These are all instances of the less weighty types of international collaboration, but they may easily add up to a significant increment in power. Smooth international cooperation is hardly thinkable without a daily interchange of courtesies and favors. The good will that officials of international organizations display toward certain states is another instance of external power-input.

3. Supporting actions of individuals and groups in other states. Such activities range from those taken within the legal

and constitutional framework of a state, through actions that are not illegal and yet are disapproved of by the greater part of the community, to illegal acts in open opposition to the established order, such as subversion and armed resistance. Instances of such actions are not rare. Communist parties all over the world support the foreign policy of the Soviet Union in return for whatever Soviet support they may obtain for their own aspirations, and they seek to influence their own governments in its favor. But support for Soviet policy can be gathered from an even wider circle than that comprised of Party members and their declared followers. The Communist Party organizes "front" oragnizations that, on specific issues, seeks the support of wider sections of the population. Thus the World Peace Movement attempts to appeal to the not-inconsiderable world pacifist sentiment and tries to rally it in support of Soviet aims. But activities of citizens of one state in support of the policy of another state are not confined to Communists. In the past, British liberals frequently attempted, and succeeded in their attempts, to influence the government to act on behalf of some threatened or oppressed friends—e.g., on behalf of the Turks against Russia in 1853–55. The activities of friends of Nationalist China in the United States, and of the organizations of the so-called hyphenated Americans on behalf of their countries of origin, are other examples of this type of action. Important services may also be obtained from exiles and refugees from a state whose policy another state wishes to change.

4. Receipt of matériel and equipment from another state. The supply of goods and equipment may be either directly or indirectly compensated. Pure barter and simple trade exchange fall into the first category; foreign aid, reparations, and other tributes and supplies from state-owned overseas enterprises come under the second heading. It should be noted in this connection that foreign trade cannot be considered in isolation from foreign policy: Imports of goods are a service

rendered by one state to another. They are part of the recipient state's power-input, and they must be suitably compensated, usually in the form of exports. There are times when imports cannot be paid for with exports; such a situation gives rise to foreign aid if the prospective donor state considers it in accordance with its interests to make up the recipient's power-input in such a manner. These statements must, it is true, be approached with caution. Not all power-inputs are affected in the same way by international trade; trade cannot always be considered as a contribution to power-input. In countries where state economic activities cover a wide field—as they do, for example, in the Communist nations—any hitch in foreign trade has an immediate impact on power-input. In countries where trade does not to any significant extent come within the sphere of state activities (and the number of these states is growing smaller), foreign trade nevertheless influences power-input in an indirect manner. Were it not so, there would be little point in economic blockade.

5. Services of power-resources of other states. There are many ways in which the power-resources of one state can be of service to the government of another state. The value of such services derives from the nature of resources: Their creation involves power-output—that is, expenditure of time and effort. Instead of going to the trouble of creating new power-resources, policy-makers may find it more convenient to use those of their allies. Furthermore, the advantages conferred by the use of the power-resources of friendly states are frequently unique, since similar facilities may not be obtainable from other sources. Thus, during the war in the Atlantic, the Azores were the only point from which the safety of shipping in that area could be ensured. There are many kinds of power-resources, both human and nonhuman, that can be of use to other states. First, territory: Allied territory can for many purpose be considered as an extension of the ego-state's territory. Parts of that territory may be used as bases for the armed forces; the free-

dom of movement, not only of troops, but of all other foreign-policy organizations, is thus enlarged. A state will also benefit from installations situated on that territory: Harbor facilities can be used by its fleet, and airports by its air force; radio stations can transmit its broadcasts overseas; and its personnel can use buildings and housing facilities. There are industrial and technical opportunities: The industrial capacity of a friendly state can be used for the manufacture of weapons or equipment; industrial processes and technical know-how can be learned from it. To some extent, the reserves of an ally can be called upon in case of need. Raw-material resources are among the other valuable assets a friendly country can provide. A friendly population can be used in the construction and servicing of overseas bases. An ally's institutionalized training facilities, such as universities, research institutes, staff colleges, and officers' schools, can be of invaluable assistance when a country wishes to train its cadres or inject some new ideas into its personnel. Finally, there are the advantages to be gained from the accumulated experience and established connections of an ally who is less well provided with other types of resources, but more mature in his experience in international life.

These are the five main varieties of services that can be obtained from other states in return for current compensating action. Other external power-input is received as the result of past efforts; these are the fruits of external power-resources.

The present and future behavior of a state are judged in relation to its past actions; these actions leave a deposit in the minds of onlookers, and whatever the exact truth of such memories may be, they influence the reactions to its present policies. These are the advantages of having a good name and a good reputation: a reputation for being powerful, a reputation for keeping one's word, a reputation for fair dealings with small allies. Thus, for instance, the word of the British Government carries considerable weight because in the past that word has been adhered to. One reason why the British declaration on the guarantee to the European Defense Community was received with particular satisfaction in Western Germany was due, as the German official spokesman put it, to the way Britain had honored her guarantees to Belgium in 1914, and to Poland in 1939. Such reputation is invaluable in the daily dealings of diplomacy, for it can remove the hard rocks of distrust on which any conference, any series of negotiations, may founder. A reputation for power may render the actual exercise of power unnecessary.

Some states feel obliged to perform services for other states as the result of past services that they have obtained from them. In a common war, or in any other common enterprise, a situation in which one state is felt to have made a contribution larger than that of another gives it an advantage in any negotiations it may choose to open. In postwar negotiations, the pull that any one state is able to exercise is to some extent determined by the measure of sacrifices it has contributed to the common cause. There was a feeling of indebtedness to France after World War I, because of the two million French dead. The importance of such a feeling should not be overemphasized, but it is there and represents another point that negotiators can make when they state their case.

Another part of external power-input is the benefits arising out of obligations or commitments of other states. These may include provisions for the payment of reparations, grants of exclusive rights and privileges in trade and industry or, in the sphere of defense, treaty obligations limiting or prohibiting armaments, prohibition or limitation of some kinds of industrial development (e.g., shipbuilding, air transport, atomic energy), control over fortifications in parts of the national territory, and any other pledges or obligations either increasing the power-input of one state or reducing that of another.

The increment in the power of a friendly state that is traceable to past aid must also be considered in this analysis.

Foreign aid has frequently been advocated as an investment. In so far as judicious assistance permanently augments the position of a friendly country, and if that country remains friendly, foreign aid creates power-resources from which the donor state derives important benefits. Even more important, perhaps, the present number of allies, the very fact of having allies, may depend on the amount of aid and other support given in the past. Thus the present and future usefulness of Greece and Turkey to the United States may be largely the result of the timely assistance given them in the immediate postwar years.

Accounts of external power-input must include mention of power-input obtained as the result of incurring liabilities and of making promises. This is the case of states living on diplomatic credit, as it were. Power-liabilities may be conceived of as the obverse of external power-resources. One state's external power-inputs are, to another state, expenditures consumed in the creation of external power-resources. A state may seek to create external power-assets—for instance, by giving military aid to an ally. The future services that it expects to receive as the result of its power-outputs are, for example, armed assistance in the event of a war. From the point of view of the recipient state, the military aid it receives (as part of its power-input) is due to the implicit or explicit understanding or obligation that in the future it will be ready to pursue certain specified policies—i.e., that it will come to the assistance of another state. The recipient state thus obtains power-input by incurring a liability or by making a promise. This common type of diplomatic situation is touched upon in one account of the reasons for which an American Secretary of State urged support of the British proposals for an Open Door declaration: Secretary Hay thought that "we were unwise not to be sympathetic to the British in a situation where we might help them and perhaps thereby build up a sort of diplomatic credit on which we could draw later."[5] He wanted to build up "diplomatic credit" for the United States, while Britain, in accepting American support, would have augmented its momentary power-input by incurring a liability.

The personal ability of policy-makers, and the adeptness with which they perform the tasks of policy-making, are unquestionably a component of the power-input of a state. Since some are better at their job than others, the acquisition of capable policy-makers represents an important increment in the power-input of every state. Lastly, policy-makers receive some power-input, not in connection with any specific reward or service, past, present, or future, but on the strength of the confidence placed in them as the custodians of the general interests of the community.

The outline of the components of power-input is thus concluded. At first glance the variety of these components may appear confusing, yet they are easily grasped if it is remembered that this classification relies on three basic distinctions: that between internal and external power-input; that between human and nonhuman components of power; and, third, on the concept of power as a return for present, past, or future actions. Whoever accepts that these distinctions reveal significant aspects of power and adopts them for purposes of analysis will arrive at a similar outline, whatever the differences in detail.

The justification for a lengthy treatment of this subject is the fundamental importance of power-input to the remainder of the argument. The basic categories in terms of which problems of power must be discussed—power-input and power-output, power-resources and liabilities—have now been introduced. The immediate aim has been to provide a framework of ideas with whose help the power-input of a state may be appraised in the context of foreign-policy analysis, to provide

[5] George F. Kennan, *American Diplomacy, 1900–1950* (Chicago: University of Chicago Press, 1951), p. 27.

not an inventory of the power-input of any one state, but a number of rubrics under which the components of the power-input of a state may be entered and thus summed up more easily. The wider purpose of this discussion has been to bring the abstract concept of power-input to life and demonstrate its empirical relevance and the insights it is capable of yielding, and, furthermore, to lay out the conceptual framework for the systematic discussion of changes in power-input and of such problems as how power-input can be increased or measured.

Before focusing our attention on power-outputs, we may wish to recall their place in relation to power-inputs and in the structure of foreign policy.

From the point of view of power, the political system may be regarded as a machine that is fed with fuels and materials, and from which issues an assortment of "policy products." The "foreign-policy machine" is fed with power-inputs, and it transforms them into power-outputs: those expenditures of power that are required for the protection of the interests of the community. Schematically, the inputs and outputs of power may be represented in the following way:

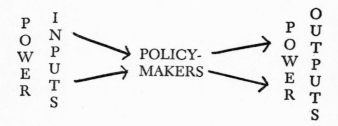

This sketch does not purport to prove anything, but it does illustrate the manner in which the relation between power-input and power-output is conceived of here. It makes it easier to visualize the close relationship existing between power-input and power-output and suggests that power-output cannot exceed power-input, which is merely another way of saying that the foreign-policy operations of a state are limited by the amount of power at its disposal. There must always be a formal equality between power-input and power-output; any discrepancy between them is traceable to growth or decline in power-resources. Since a state cannot live beyond its means forever, or for any significant period, equilibrating processes set in that adjust power-output to power-input and vice versa. The function of government is to provide an adjustment mechanism between these two elements of foreign policy, so as to ensure an efficient transformation of inputs into outputs.

Analysis of Power-output

The distinction between power-input and power-output reflects the fact that in dealing with power we have to study two processes that are in many ways separate—one of them centered around the problem of "getting" power, the other focused on the question of "using" power. Both of them, however, are no more than two ways of looking at the same phenomenon.

The train of reasoning about power-output might well begin with the statement that all foreign-policy operations—that is, all measures directed toward the outside world and aimed at changing the foreign policies of other states—involve power-output. In other words, there can be no state action in the international field that does not, in one form or another, constitute a drain on power. This proposition restates the previous assertions that all outputs have a power aspect and that, furthermore, all actions have means, or power, as one of their minimum elements. All foreign policy requires power-input, which is to say that power must be provided if foreign policy is to be followed at all; every foreign-policy operation (output) involves the use, or misuse, of that power. But resort to these axiomatic statements is not absolutely necessary, because it is clear that every foreign-policy move—be it the dispatch of a note, the world tour of a minister, the grant of aid, or the movement of an army—requires effort and expense. These actions involve, first of all, claims on the time and energy of men in foreign-policy organizations; these organizations, in turn, require the supporting services of nonhuman elements and of power-resources. Diversion of resources, human and nonhuman, from other uses is a necessary feature of all foreign-policy moves, and resources are power. In short, there is no action without power.

With the help of this notion, it is possible to gain a theoretical approach to the problem of giving an *ex post* account of the foreign-policy operations of a state. Since all foreign-policy moves necessitate an exertion of power, there is a corresponding action for every power-output. Thus an account of power-outputs presents by implication a complete picture of foreign-policy operations in their "power" aspect. Power, and its exertion, are what may be called the tangible or observable elements of foreign policy; more so than objectives, the components of power are things one can "put one's finger on." Changes in power-output may be identified more easily than changes in other elements involved in foreign policy. On general grounds, it can thus be claimed that a picture of the foreign-policy operations of a state can be inferred from an account of its power-output.

This generalization must be qualified from two points of view. For one, what may be called "basic" power-outputs account for an important proportion of the yearly power-output. Every state must maintain an administrative structure of government, a rudimentary network of diplomatic outposts, and at least the skeleton of an army and other services. The basic power-outputs for the maintenance of these organizations are the consequence of a state's existence rather than of its pursuit of certain policies. But all that goes beyond these rudiments, all "policy" power-outputs—and, as a rule, the larger the state, the more there is of this nonbasic power-output—

must be capable of being allocated to specific policies. The criterion of basic power-output is its absolute necessity to the existence of an organized state; thus the account of power-output, to be genuinely illuminating, must draw a distinction between *basic* and *policy* outputs and must concentrate on the latter.

The second qualification concerns the fact that foreign policies call for varying amounts of power-outputs. While fighting a war might absorb the energies of millions of men, conducting an important series of negotiations may require no more than a few hundred people and a correspondingly small cost in terms of the other components of power. The significance of an action is not necessarily exhausted by the amount of power exerted in it; its meaning may be chiefly symbolic and lie in its expression of an objective, an expression of intention to act and to exert power, now or in the future. Actions of this kind, insignificant in terms of power-output, can easily be overlooked in a picture of foreign policy inferred from power-output alone.

The components of power-output may be analyzed on two levels, both related to the kind of results they produce: (1) by reference to the extent to which their beneficial effects can be located in the present or in the future or in neither; (2) by conceiving of power-output as the cost of foreign-policy operations.

First of all, power-outputs can be classified by reference to the point in time at which they are expected to produce results. On this basis, we may distinguish among current-service, future-service, and past-service power-outputs. More explicitly, some power-outputs produce immediate effects and bring immediate benefits. Others result in an accumulation of power-resources; they may be expected to produce future power-input but they bring no immediate benefit. (This future-oriented power-output we will call "power-investment.") Lastly, some components of power-output are fated not to produce any new benefits; they are necessary because of liabilities incurred in the past and correspond to benefits reaped that must now be paid for.

Of these three kinds of power-output, the first is certainly the most obvious and perhaps the least interesting: There is nothing very surprising in the observation that power is being expended in the production of concurrent benefits. "Power-output" stands for the uses to which power-input is being put; the most obvious and the most urgent of these lie in the present. Thus, for instance, a large part of the peacetime services of the armed forces is utilized in ensuring the safety of the frontiers of the state and in deterring aggressors; in wartime, in the defensive aspect of their operations, the armed forces similarly seek to ensure the country's day-to-day security. Responses to the moves of other states cannot be delayed, and the actions of other states must be met by current reactions. At any time, a state engages in a number of positive operations of its own (negotiations, disputes, aid programs, wars) and all of these demand their share of power-output. Finally, foreign-policy–making is a continuous operation, and the supply of intelligence, the upkeep of administrative machinery, and the production of information and propaganda can never be given up entirely.

All this is indeed elementary. Only one part of this power-output presents special problems to be noted at this point; these arise when a state fails to maintain its power-investment ("lives on its capital") or sacrifices some future advantage and diverts power-outflows from power-investment to current use in order to obtain some momentary benefit. This is merely another way of defining shortsightedness in foreign policy, but it does no harm to point out where it fits into our framework. There is no denying that in circumstances of great urgency, in moments of supreme crisis, governments are fully justified in drawing on any and all sources and resources to help avert the "present danger." But while these moments are very rare indeed, the temptation to augment present power-output at the expense of the future is often great, and some-times overwhelming, and it is not only the lesser men who succumb to it. How often is the only result of a "diplomatic victory," apart from a little applause at home, the unnecessary humiliation of the opponent and the arousing of his hatred? Or, alternatively, a promise may be made that cannot possibly be fulfilled, but is bound to restrict future freedom of action, and indeed, as soon as the immediate circumstances change, is likely to prove embarrassing. In striking contrast was a World War II standing directive on British psychological warfare that stated that "nothing must be done . . . which would prejudice Government policy towards Germany after the war."

For theoretical purposes, and in the present argument, by far the most important category of power-outputs is designed to produce, and does in fact produce, future benefits. There may at this point be some uncertainty about the criterion with which to distinguish the present from the future; but there need not be any one fixed definition of "the present." It is largely a matter of the urgency of the hour. In moments of desperate need, any power-output whose beneficial effects cannot be expected to materialize until a few weeks or months have passed must be considered as belonging to the future. Thus, during the critical months that Britain lived through after the fall of France in June, 1940, supreme priority was allocated only to the construction of works that could offer effective defense against the enemy by the end of September, 1940. In more settled times, with little uncertainty or danger ahead, the present may extend to more than one or two years. The period of one year is a fairly convenient measure of the present, because state budgets are usually based on a similar time span.

The important part the services of power-resources or assets play in power-input has already been pointed out. In a certain sense it may even be argued that power-input is impossible without power-resources. Resources constitute the very backbone of power-input, and for this reason all those whose task it is to decide on how to distribute power-output, how to allocate it among the various tasks facing foreign policy, will have to face the problem of devoting a certain proportion of it to operations relating to the formation of resources. Since it is inherent in power-resources that they cannot be created immediately, efforts to accumulate resources are identical with the part of power-output that is intended to produce, and that results in the production of, future benefits. From now onward we shall call this operation—the part of power-output that is to produce future benefits—the process of accumulating power or, in short, "power-investment." Power-investment deserves sustained theoretical attention because existing accounts of foreign policy are excessively concerned with the study of the past and pay insufficient regard to inquiries into the methods of better exploring the future. There is no danger of falling into that error when studying the processes of power-investment. Anybody facing the problem of allocating a part of power-output to investment purposes must at the same time attempt to relate this problem to the future of foreign policy and to anticipate the actions of others.

In the section dealing with components of power-input, we have noted various types of power-resources: in use and in reserve; internal and external; and human and nonhuman. As regards output, the two main kinds of power-investment we shall discuss will be the maintenance of existing resources and the creation of new ones.

1. Maintenance of existing power-resources. At any given time, the government and the community dispose of a definite amount of power-assets, a finite quantity of resources. This stock of power is in hand, ready to be drawn upon. And yet, although its long lease of life is one of its most striking char-

acteristics (this length of life being dependent on the nature of the particular asset), another of its features is hardly less essential or important: If it is not regularly attended to, such an asset wears out and deteriorates.

There is little permanence in the apparent solidity of national and governmental resources. All assets require constant care and occasional replacement. It may be worth recalling that victorious nations in particular are in the habit of resting on their laurels and thinking that the armies, the organization, and the alliances that produced victory are bound to do the same the next time without additional effort. Foreign-policy organizations—military, diplomatic, or propaganda—once brought to a high pitch of efficiency, will not remain there unless constant attention is paid to them; unless they receive a steady flow of replacements and their appropriate share of national brainpower; unless they are kept in constant training and adapt themselves steadily to changing conditions of national and international life. Nor will these organizations be of much value if the equipment they use wears out or becomes outdated; if reserves are allowed to reach a dangerously low level; if industry and science, on which they must rely, lag behind in the technological race. Just as existing equipment must be maintained in sufficient numbers and readiness and promptly replaced once it has become unable to fulfill its tasks efficiently, the external power-resources of a state—alliances and international good will—will not endure unless they are cared for like a tender plant. Thus a portion of power-output must be allocated to the support of traditional friendships and international comity.

Apart from conscious policy decisions, on which it is better not to rely entirely, what are the processes operating to ensure the maintenance of power-resources? The high national standing and prestige in the eyes of the policy-makers and of the wider public enjoyed by diplomatic, military, and other foreign-policy organizations are a counterweight to the tendency of statesmen to live for the moment. The organizations' advice need not always be heeded, but it must always be the subject of serious discussion; though little can be done if the policy-makers themselves fail to recommend the appropriate measures. What is more, there should be men and groups whose special task is to see to it that national assets are receiving the proper attention, that they are being suitably maintained and replaced—men whose income and standing depend on the fact that this happens.

Throughout this discussion, it has been assumed that power-resources continue to be required for the successful conduct of foreign policy. But existing resources need not be maintained at all cost, nor must all of them be maintained. They are useful as long as they yield services that are required for an effective pursuit of governmental policy. As soon as those services are no longer required, and if there is no likelihood of their being needed in the foreseeable future—which is an important "if"—the need to maintain the resources that produce them disappears, too. Thus, when political understanding with the United States and deterioration of relations with Germany caused the withdrawal of the British naval squadron from the West Indies in the first decade of the twentieth century, the necessity of maintaining naval bases and large docks in that area vanished, too. Or, if an alignment against a third state results in military and other cooperation, the need to maintain such mutual aid will disappear once the third state has been finally defeated.

2. Formation of new power-resources. While it may seem more or less a matter of common sense or routine to keep existing resources in a good state of repair, a decision to embark on the creation of additional power-resources usually comes under closer scrutiny. This is of course the reverse of the decision—just mentioned—to stop maintaining part of existing power-resources. Let us elaborate a little further.

Let us first look at the conditions under which power-investment becomes *possible* at all, as distinct from being *desirable*. Power-investment consists in allocating a part of power-output to the creation of new resources. The most important feature of the process is the fact that the future advantages that are to result from power-investment can only be had at the price of reducing current output. Since at no time can more than a certain proportion of power-output be assigned to power-investment, it follows that the size of investment is directly dependent on the size of power-input. The smaller the power-input, the smaller must power-investment be. New power-resources (including reserves) can thus be created in only two ways: (1) through an increase in power-input, or (2) through the sacrifice of existing outputs (policies). Either process requires sacrifice—directly, in order to put a larger amount of resources at the disposal of the policy-makers; or indirectly, because of the abandonment of other policies and the loss of benefits flowing from it. Thus, armament against a hostile state may be achieved either by increasing taxes, loans, conscription, foreign aid, or by giving up alternative policies, such as an active policy against another state.

Mention must now be made of a further limiting factor on power-investment—namely, the quality of power-input as contrasted with its mere size. Power-investment, particularly in its more elaborate phases, is impossible unless the directors of policy possess a certain amount of skill, and unless this skill is also present in the society at large. Since the main types of power-resources are skilled and trained men, territory and equipment, and allies, the corresponding specific facilities for their production would consist of training establishments with a supply of experienced men who can transfer their experience to their pupils; an industrial structure able to produce the necessary equipment for foreign-policy organizations (weapons, planes, ships, etc.); and the other facilities that go to improve the functioning of these organizations (such as transport and communication networks) and to encourage the exploitation of a territory's potentialities. Finally, the formation of alliances demands a great deal of diplomatic skill: foresight in obtaining and preserving allies, in maintaining them as strong as one's power-output will allow and other conditions will require, as well as the ability to offer them other advantages. These facilities will not be readily available if the national society itself does not possess a large degree of division of labor and dispose of certain wider national assets. Power-investment presupposes pre-existing power-resources with whose help the process must take place: Thus, the training of men requires men who are already trained, the production of equipment demands equipment to produce that equipment. Allies can be had and kept only if they are offered benefits in exchange, and states that do not dispose of some power-resources are unlikely to be able to do so. The generalization may therefore be made that the smaller the power-resources of a nation, the more difficult the process of investment is likely to prove.

We have just described the broad framework within which power-investment is *possible* at all; we must now examine the desirability of this process or, in other words, the sort of context in which it becomes *necessary*.

It is the fundamental advantage of power-assets that policies that could not be executed at all without the services of power-assets, or could be accomplished only imperfectly, can with their help be entered upon and successfully completed or conducted more efficiently. Power-resources enable a state to do more, better. Thus, for instance, a state cannot think of protecting its interests overseas effectively or of projecting its will across the seas without a navy, including a merchant marine; and a navy cannot be constructed overnight, or even over a period of a few years. Power-investment in the form of ship construction and training of naval personnel in due course enlarges power-input and puts the state in a position to embark upon policies it could not have pursued previously (except with the aid of allies). Furthermore, having a navy may enable a state to carry out policies at the cost of a smaller power-output—that is, more efficiently.

Power-investment thus (1) makes new actions possible and (2) increases the efficiency of actions. Accordingly, investment should be undertaken whenever (1) future policies demand it, and (2) greater efficiency is desirable and attainable.

We are next confronted with the second determinant of power-investment (the first being the size of power-input): the objectives of foreign policy. Discussed at greater length elsewhere, objectives can here be defined as conceptions of the future, desirable behavior of other states. This concept of objectives links up easily with that of power-investment—above all, because all power is instrumental in the achievement of objectives, but particularly because objectives and power-investment are both oriented toward the future.

To say that a state has interests and objectives of policy means that it must, both at present and in the future, act to influence other states. Such future action requires power-resources as one of its components. Changes in objectives therefore inevitably result in changes in power-investment, new objectives creating new investment needs.

How does this work in practice? A typical case would proceed somewhat as follows: The actions of state B convince state A that friendship with B is no longer to be taken for granted and that war is no longer inconceivable. War becomes a risk to be ensured against and A's foreign-policy organizations now go ahead with preparations for such an eventuality. The general staffs start drawing up plans for troop dispositions in case of a conflict. If the two states have a land frontier in common, fortifications may be erected along it; if they are not adjacent, consideration will have to be given to the defense of those sectors of the national territory that are vulnerable to B's attacks. Special equipment of a kind suited to operations on B's territory will be put into production. Selected personnel will be instructed in the language and geography of country B. Steps will be taken to enlarge the flow and accumulated stock of information about B. In the external field, prospective allies against B will be supported, in anticipation of the services they may be called upon to give in case of war. Such activities amount to creating new resources, the necessary components of possible military operations.

All types of changes of objective, such as those arising out of the attainment or abandonment of a previous objective or the adoption of a new one, bring about changes in the pattern of power-investment. Thus, if radio propaganda is to be expanded, the broadcasting organization must be enlarged and new transmitters commissioned; if foreign broadcasts are to be jammed, jamming organizations and stations must be set up. This is, however, only a statement of a long-term trend. Changes in subsidiary objectives, such as those implicit in a temporary move on the diplomatic scene, may be accommodated out of "reserve capacity" and will scarcely influence the fundamental investment process.

The execution of changes in power-investment is rarely simple. In American practice, the State Department comes closest to being the agency whose function it is to define the objectives of U.S. foreign policy. Power-investment, on the other hand, devolves upon a number of government departments and the carrying out of changes in power-investment according to variations in policies naturally encounters obstacles. Within armed forces, it is the normal duty of a general staff to plan for the future; but despite attempts to reproduce the general-staff pattern in foreign ministries—e.g., the Policy Planning Staff of the State Department—the continuous matching of objectives with power-investment still remains to be adopted as a conscious operating procedure. It is a task that only the policy-makers themselves can tackle with complete authority, because it touches upon the most urgent concerns of foreign policy. The responsibility for co-ordinating all foreign-affairs activities, and therefore for co-ordinating present and future activities, must ultimately rest with the President.

Greater efficiency should be the constant aim of policy-makers. The efficiency of foreign policy can be said to have improved if increased tasks can be fulfilled with a given amount of power-output, or if a reduced power-output performs an equal number of tasks. Improvements in efficiency are the result of investment. Investment represents forethought, planning, and careful preparation. Forethought and planning are not achieved without effort; the resources expended on them are the cost of power-investment. Applied to every policy, forethought and preparation yield benefits in terms of reduced power-output. Phases during which a state engages in many foreign-policy operations are usually times of the creation of power-investment associated with new policies, times in which little attention is paid to efficiency. But these phases are usually followed by periods of passivity, devoted to "the licking of wounds" or "the enjoyment of the fruits of victory." It is at such times of consolidation that efficiency becomes more important than grand enterprise. A power that neglects the investment required in constant efforts to keep the quality of its operations on a level with that of its com-petitors is truly declining.

What kinds of efficiency do we have in mind when we talk of foreign policy? First, there is the competence, experience, and quality of training of personnel (both active and reserve). These can be improved either by further training or by re-placement with more qualified personnel. There is also the efficiency of equipment: that of the armed forces, the indus-trial equipment of the nation, and the technical apparatus of the state. Technical innovations and scientific advance, com-bined with the progress of other states, keep up a steady pres-sure for improving power-resources in this field. Research in the field of weapons development has become a familiar feature of the military scene. In the external field, there is always room for improvement in the quality of cooperation, communication, and consultation with friendly states. The quality of a nation's policy-makers and their advisers and critics, their familiarity with foreign-policy operations, and their ability to inspire those on whose behalf they are acting are other factors of efficiency.

There is no denying that the problem of estimating efficiency of foreign policy is far from easy. Public criticism, whenever it is allowed, keeps some check on the efficiency of foreign operations, though in some countries there is a tendency to frown upon criticisms of this particular aspect of national life. Internal and international competition and comparisons between policy-makers are a powerful mechanism working for efficiency in foreign policy. But whatever the difficulties of comparing or estimating efficiency, there are always fields in which the application of foresight would improve the quality of a country's foreign policy and in which investment is therefore justified.

Future policy requirements and the demands of efficiency are the two most compelling reasons why countries should invest in power. Power-resources are such an indivisible part of power and of policy that almost any power-investment might appear good in itself. But this is not because the process is very strongly oriented to the future. This orientation is at once the source of its importance and the reason for its riskiness. Power-investment is based on an estimate of future policies and a comparison of present and future results of power-output: The estimate may be wrong and the sacrifice incurred may have been in vain. Thus, if it is desired to create external assets through a foreign-assistance program, the risk that the recipient state may turn hostile must be taken. Decisions to concentrate on the strategic air forces at the expense of ground armies involve similar risks. Finally, though

efficiency often seems desirable for its own sake, the absolute
pursuit of efficiency in one field of national life at the expense
of other fields may also be misguided. Like all the great
decisions of politics, the decision to invest in power is therefore fraught with risks and dangers.

Foreign policy, like other forms of human activity, takes
place in a continuum in which present actions project their
effects on the future and in which the past casts its shadow
on the present. Let us now consider the ways in which some
power-outputs help to reduce this unavoidable burden of the
past.

Power liabilities[6] are limitations imposed by a state's past
policies upon its freedom to allocate resources. They are
part of the heritage any state must carry along with its assets.
For instance, many of the difficulties experienced by the
German Federal Republic when it first entered the international scene were due to its being the successor to Hitler's
Germany. There are three main kinds of liabilities: (1) obligations accruing as the result of benefits received, (2) past
weakness, and (3) bad reputation.

Any but the most rudimentary forms of human intercourse,
within and between states, take place within an established
framework of agreements, promises, and expectations. Obligations assumed under agreements that have not yet been dis-
charged are therefore a very important part of national
liabilities.

Internally, the most obvious instance of liabilities resulting in power-output is the servicing of internal "indebtedness." A government is expected to be loyal to its personnel
and to extend care and protection to veterans of past wars and
their dependents. Governments also attempt to make good the
promises they have given in the past, rashly though they may

[6] Power-resources are the present, favorable result of past outputs (power-
investment); power liabilities are the present, unfavorable results of past power-
inputs (or of past postponement of power-outputs).

have been made—for instance, at election times—and to satisfy groups to whose support they owe their position in power. Externally, the government is caught in a network of obligations deriving both from the treaties, conventions, and agreements limiting its freedom of action in a variety of fields and from the rules of international law. Alliances, too, have in them an element of liability: the obligation to accept the interests of one's allies as if they were one's own and to work for their attainment.

No less important are the obligations, implicit though they may be, that are incurred as the result of accepting foreign aid and support. In his "Pacificus" and "Americanus" articles, Alexander Hamilton asserted that in foreign policy "there is no room for gratitude . . . among nations. . . . Such occasions . . . perhaps never occur." But Hamilton was taking part in a debate about entering the war against Britain on the grounds of American gratitude to France. In that case, the other interests of the United States pointed too strongly in another direction for gratitude to hold sway. Gratitude nevertheless may sometimes be a ground on which power-output is incurred. To give only one example, when Bismarck, in 1863–64, was helping the Czar to suppress the Polish rising, he was clearly counting on benefiting from Russia's friendly attitude when he engaged in later conflicts. In 1870, Russia did not intervene in the Franco-German War, and the Czar's gratitude is among the reasons usually given for this. There may be cases, like the one Hamilton was arguing about, in which gratitude is so clearly opposed to other interests that it cannot be expressed in action. Yet it cannot be said that gratitude is never operative; in ordinary human relations, the function of gratitude and the emotions associated with it is to consolidate certain types of relations; failure to be grateful generates resentment. The same considerations apply in international relations: Foreign aid or support is not charity, for it is given either in the pursuit of a direct object or in the interest of strengthening an alliance. In the latter case in particular, gratitude is significant because it lends stability to the relationship. Aid is given in the expectation that the recipient state is and will remain an ally; the feeling of gratitude thus generated helps to ensure the preservation of the alliance.

Power-inputs attributable to past weakness are in some ways an extension of the preceding argument, since the need to cooperate, to seek allies, arises precisely because the resources of most states are insufficient in relation to the tasks facing them—in other words, because most states are weak. But there may be a difference between obligations undertaken more or less voluntarily as the price of cooperation (such as the subordination of part of a nation's armed forces to an allied supreme command) and obligations that are imposed (such as reparations and other consequences of defeat, or the disadvantages derived from satellite status). Internally, cases of power-output resulting from past weakness may occur when the government is the prisoner of one particular section of the community—the community being all those whose interests the government is charged to protect. Weak governments, whether too weak either to attain office unaided or to remain in power securely, are never masters in their own houses. Externally, there is the case of military defeat. A defeated state performs services for the benefit of the victorious power: delivery of reparations, maintenance of occupation troops, temporary or permanent loss of manpower and territory. There is also partial, and sometimes complete, loss of influence and capacity to act on the international scene, with a consequent inability to protect the country's interests. Power-input is significantly reduced and part of power-output is mortgaged to pay the price of defeat.

Some defeats may be transitory; other defeats (or mere weakness in certain circumstances) may bring about permanent subjection or reduction to satellite status. The price of such subjection is the payment of a tribute to avoid even greater hardships. As the result of subjection, the power-output of the satellite state—for instance, its armies—is used to further the interests of the dominant state. Its foreign trade, as a rule, will be transacted on terms that are particularly advantageous to the controlling power. If the process goes far enough, there may be no point in talking about a separate foreign policy.

Finally, there is the case of bad reputation. Such reputation is usually the result of past behavior—for instance, behavior that throws doubt on the state's reliability as an ally, on its willingness to keep promises, or that evidences contempt for decency and humanity in international relations. The past is not easy to live down, for nations do not easily forget. Some states attain quick results without heeding the wishes of their friends, riding roughshod over their several interests. Such behavior may bring spectacular results, but has to be paid for some day in the mistrust and hostility it inevitably arouses.

Costs of Policy

The analysis so far has demonstrated the magnitude of the claim that the future and the past have upon governmental power-output. But since the policy of a state consists of a number of different actions or operations, the study of power-output can yield light on another significant aspect of foreign policy: the costs and other effects of particular actions making up foreign-policy operations. The costs of a foreign-policy operation are the proportion of total power-output expended in the pursuit of that operation.

Our purpose in studying the costs of policies is to help improve policy-making and its criticism; mainly, to enable policy-makers and their critics to evaluate past and future policies more rationally. If the cost of an action is known, it can be compared with the gains derived from it (gains being defined as attained objectives) and with the other effects of action.[7]

Attempts to estimate power-output and costs proceed from the assumption that power is homogeneous, "an indivisible whole." If power is homogeneous, parts of it must be interchangeable. Elements of power committed to one particular policy can be transferred to other policies. Conversely, an increase in one specific element of power means an increase in the over-all ability to act.

To illustrate, imagine an atomic bomb hitting a foreign ministry, resulting in a total loss of personnel, documents, and equipment. Grave though the disaster would be, it would not entail a cessation of all foreign relations. In part, the ministry's functions would be taken over by existing organizations, such as cabinet offices and other departments. A new organization would soon be set up, drawing on personnel from missions abroad, from other ministries, and from the services, capable of performing its functions with comparatively reasonable efficiency. But the initial disorganization and chaos, the delays, the withdrawal of personnel and resources from other tasks, would cause a decrease in power-input. Conversely, the acquisition of an atomic weapon means not only an increase in power to inflict destruction, but also an increase in total power through the release of resources from other tasks.

The interchangeability of power components and the proc-

[7] There are three other effects that an action may have in respect to power: It may (1) increase the power-input of other states—for instance, allies (or reduce their power-output); (2) reduce the power-input of other states—e.g., that of hostile states; or (3) increase the power-input (or reduce the power-output) of one's own state. A fourth effect might be an increase in power-output of one's own state, defined as the costs of action. In so far as some characteristic policy patterns produce effects that pronouncedly fall into one of these categories, they could be classified accordingly. Some such patterns, like support or aid to other states, clearly increase their power-input. Blockade, international war, and fifth-column activities are drastic means of reducing power-input. On the other hand, deals, bargains, or negotiated settlements may secure an increase in power. Other types of policies may not fall so happily into one of these categories; often, their effects belong to more than one of them. (On the effects of policies and on methods of changing policies, see Part IV.)

esses to which it gives rise is the major justification for a general concept of power. But this is by no means the whole story. Far from being completely interchangeable, some components of power are irreplaceable, in the sense that without them a state could not exert any influence at all. Although some components of power-input are in part interchangeable, no state exists that would dispense with any one of them entirely; no organization can exist without the services of human beings and/or without supplies of matériel. No state does, or can, rely entirely on its own power. A state without a structure of assets and a minimum network of obligations, promises, and expectations is not conceivable. That is why, strictly speaking, one cannot compare the diverse elements of power or measure them with a common yardstick. But one should be able to arrive at a compromise taking into account the fact that interchangeability is a matter of degree.

Basically, all power consists of capacity for organized action in the service of foreign policy. Since, however, a general yardstick for the measurement of power yet remains to be devised, we must rest content with partial indexes. The military power of a state serves as one such practical indication, money as another. Stalin's celebrated query: "How many divisions has the Pope?" indicates one criterion for measuring power. There is some justification for using this particular yardstick, because an army division is the basic independent organization, and also because military power can be considered the most fundamental part of a state's power. The query should be enlarged to mean also "How many divisions can the state organize, and how many can it maintain over a prolonged period?" But such computation would clearly not be enough. The Pope himself, although he has no divisions, can still bring his influence to bear in a variety of situations. There are other components besides divisions making up the power of a state. Attempts to estimate power in terms of money reflect the partial truth that money is a convenient yardstick for measuring the value of goods and services and some aspects of power. But there are components of power, such as alliances and the services of the armed forces, that cannot meaningfully be expressed in terms of money. An adequate level of national production, which can be expressed in terms of money, is no substitute for divisions or allies. Money, too, is only a makeshift indicator.

The significance of costs lies in the uses to which that particular power-output could have been put had it been decided to pursue an alternative policy. The sacrifice involved in pursuing one particular policy at the expense of another is equal to the value of the objectives whose attainment had to be given up or postponed. No state's resources are unlimited: The task of statesmen is to distribute the available power among the most urgent objectives. Even powerful states like the United States are faced with decisions as to whether to send more aid to Western Europe or to Asia. Thus, it is entirely possible that the United States could equip five additional French divisions for West European defense only at the cost of sacrificing the training and equipping of more South Korean troops able to replace American troops in the Korean War.

The extent of the sacrifice depends on whether resources engaged in the pursuance of one policy can readily be used to further another policy. Returning to the previous example, it might perhaps have been argued that the type of equipment and supplies used for forming additional divisions came from stocks suitable only for the European theater of operations and could not have been utilized to equip Korean troops. In that case, the cost or sacrifice incurred in forming the French divisions was small, provided that no other uses could have been found for that equipment. This is, however, unlikely; other uses are nearly always open—for instance, equipping Italian or Belgian troops or keeping stocks up to the required level.

Considerations of interchangeability represent one part of the problem of estimating costs: They indicate the importance or value of the power-output sacrificed. But here we face another problem: how to determine the amount of power-output attributable to a given policy (bearing in mind that such cost will not show the expense of "basic" power-output).

To study the cost of foreign policies one should conceive of power as being distributed among a variety of uses. The classification of these uses and their number will depend on the purpose to which this information is to be put. Broadly speaking, these uses can be ordered according to pattern, agents, or objectives.

For some purposes it may be necessary to ascertain the division of power-output among policy patterns such as military operations, foreign aid, broadcasting to other countries, etc. Such a classification accords with the information available—for instance, in budget statements or in other sources of government statistics. Power-output can fairly easily be allocated to each of these broad patterns (for example, the United States Strategic Bombing Survey sought to determine the cost of the strategic bombing of Germany), and certain conclusions may be drawn from the proportion of output going into each of them. However, this type of arrangement of power-outputs does not make possible a comparison of costs incurred and results achieved.

Secondly, we can conceive of policy costs being incurred by a number of "agents"—heads of government departments, institutions, and organizations; military commanders; or governors of certain areas. We may wish to know the amount of power allocated to each agent in order to judge his efficiency or to define his responsibility. Indeed, to some extent we may always have to classify costs in terms of agents, because of the need to allocate responsibility and its corollary, blame and praise.

The most important method of defining policies for the

purpose of ascertaining costs is a classification in terms of objectives. Costs incurred in the pursuance of one objective must be grouped together in order to determine the power-output consequent upon that pursuit. They may then be contrasted with gains achieved, including the extent of achievement of the original objective. Difficulties arise here because objectives may frequently be a matter of speculation for the outside observer and may be uncertain even to the executors of policy; furthermore, actions are often what might be called multipurpose operations, in which it is almost impossible to allocate costs among the various objectives. While the first difficulty might be somewhat diminished as the result of increasing study and understanding of objectives, it is unlikely to disappear altogether, and the second difficulty is certain to persist.

The problem of determining cost should thus be couched in terms of determining the power-output expended for a certain objective. If, for instance, the objective of the United States is preventing the Western sectors of Berlin from falling under Soviet control, then the problem will be to find the American power-output necessary to keep West Berlin under Western influence. In 1948, that included the cost of maintaining American organizations whose task it was to ensure Berlin's security: American army units, air forces protecting the air approaches to the city, parts of the occupation staffs in Berlin and Western Germany, etc. The efforts of diplomats in negotiating a settlement with the Soviets might also be estimated. The air-lift itself was a spectacular operation that supplied aid to Berlin's population and made use of the considerable American power-resources (such as aircraft and technical resources). Retaliatory action against East Germany for blockage of eastbound traffic may also have involved some cost. What is more, in all this the United States benefited from outputs by the United Kingdom and France in support of the same objective; and when the case of the Berlin blockade came up in the United Nations, the United States received the diplomatic support of many other states.

To take another example, it may be maintained with some justice that the several million French dead and disabled were a high price to pay for winning World War I. On the other hand, Marshall Plan aid may be said to have been a cheap way of dealing with a problem that might have involved far greater power-outputs at a later stage, such as, in the extreme case, the disadvantages of fighting a war if Western Europe were under the control of a hostile power.

These examples illustrate the kind of answer that might be given to the problem of weighing costs. Basically, that answer must be given in the same terms as those in which power-input was computed, simply because one cannot measure power-output differently from power-input; they are two aspects of power. The terms are the same: human and non-human components of organizations, the use of human and nonhuman power-resources, the benefits of promises, the cost to the state (internal), and costs incurred by other states (external).

Two points remain to be made at this juncture. One is that the cost of every action will include all the elements of cost listed above: human and nonhuman power-output and resources. Since most of the actions on the international scene necessitate the cooperation of other states, there should also be an opportunity to differentiate between internal and external cost. If that scheme is kept in mind, it is easier to trace all the necessary components of the costs of any particular action.

Secondly, the query may arise: Why should the power-output of other states—for instance, that of allies—enter into the cost of a state's own achievements of objectives? One could argue that it is no concern of state A what costs state B incurs, even in the furtherance of A's objectives; in fact, the more the burden shifts onto B's shoulders, the better and cheaper it is for A. Such a line of thought is shortsighted and super-ficial. To begin with, helpful states are most frequently friendly or allied, and for that reason their power is also to some extent one's own; a reduction in their power-output indirectly means a reduction of one's own power-output. Thus their costs must be included in the computation of one's own. Equally important is the fact that power-output incurred by other states not entirely in the direct pursuance of their own objectives creates a claim on one's own behavior in the future; it creates a liability that will probably have to be honored and cannot be considered as a free gift.

The general formula for estimating the power-output of an agent over a certain period would be the following: size of power-resources, including reserves at the beginning of the period, *minus* size of resources at the end of the period *plus* power-input during the period. In other words, the power-output is identical with the agent's power-input and the dif-ference between initial and final net power-resources (since he might have lived on assets or have accumulated resources). His liabilities will also have to be considered in the calculation. This formula cannot be readily applied in cases where the agent or agency in charge of the action is hard to identify. It gives the cost of an operation rather than the cost of attaining an objective.

The above analysis was designed to show the empirical validity of the concept of power-output, and to provide the occasion for discussing some of the problems associated with its allocation. Unless a clear picture has now been acquired of power-output as the power expenses that a state incurs in the pursuit of its foreign policy, it may be difficult to follow the analysis of Part IV, which takes for granted familiarity with the four "elements" in foreign policy, including power-output and power-input.

PART THREE

ON AIMS

Part I outlined the place of the concept of "aims"—that is, "interests" and "objectives"—in the analysis of foreign policy. We are distinguishing between these two kinds of foreign-policy aims because the community's wishes with regard to foreign policy (its interests) are never fully reflected in the objectives of policy-makers, and because the complexities of the foreign-policy operations that so directly condition objectives never completely impress themselves upon interests. Although interests and objectives both belong to the species of aims or ends, they are separate variables of foreign-policy analysis, each of them subject to changes peculiar to itself.

Interests and Foreign Policy

For purposes of foreign-policy analysis, interests are the demands, wishes, and desires that pertain to the behavior of other states and that are brought to bear on policy-makers. The questions we shall attempt to answer in this section are: How can one classify interests? Whose wishes and desires are they? What is the content of these wishes and desires?

Interests are the demands of all those who have a claim on the attention of policy-makers and who can be subsumed under the general heading of "the policy-makers' community."

The community is not in most cases coextensive with the citizen body of one state. The community is both narrower and broader than the confines of a single state: Policy-makers rarely accept and uphold the demands of all the citizens of their state, and within each state there is at all times a group of people whose wishes and desires are completely ignored. Policy-makers also take account of the demands of their allies, and for this reason it is possible to say that the boundaries of their community extend beyond the frontiers of their state. The community, be it noted, is here defined by reference to its policy-makers; it is composed of all those whose interests the policy-maker is implementing. We do not say: Given a community, who are its policy-makers?—a question of greater interest to the political scientists. No, we postulate the existence of a policy-maker, and then ask: Whose interests is he serving? What is his community? The relations between the policy-makers and their community, the scope of this community, and the changes in its composition are thus of essence to the study of interests.

The community is not one of the variable "elements" of foreign policy; it is one of its structural features. Changes in the structure and composition of the community make their impact felt on foreign policy through changes in interests, which are defined as the community's demands. But in addition to being an ultimate cause or determinant of foreign policy, the community can also be conceived of as a result of foreign policy, in as much as the kind of foreign policy that the policy-maker pursues influences the composition of his community. If he pursues objectives of wide appeal, his following, his community, will expand; if the objectives of his policy are unacceptable to some of his supporters or allies, his community will contract. One of the considerations that policy-makers have to keep in mind when arriving at their decisions is the effect of their objectives on the composition of their community. The community might thus be defined as "the present result of the past pursuit of objectives." In this sense, foreign policy plays a part in the formation of communities.

It is rather important to think of the composition of the community, and hence of the "input" of interests, as being changeable. The interests that policy-makers seek to implement are never fixed, immutable, or eternal; nor are they among the inalterable facts of nature. They vary, together with the changes in the community that engenders them, and the community, in its turn, is a function of the objectives that policy-makers pursue. The community is that cluster of political groups and allied states whose interests are implemented in foreign policy, and whose present structure is the result of past objectives. It may be remarked parenthetically that, logically, the concept of community stands in the same relation to interests and objectives as power-resources do to power-input and power-output.

Inherent in the notion of community is the idea of other beings or groups who do not belong to it and who are outside it. The "in-group" presupposes, and is defined by, the "out-group." The demarcation between those who belong to the community and those who are outside it is not always sharp. Nevertheless, all those groups or states whose interests must be considered in the formation of foreign policy have their place on the spectrum that stretches between the two extremes of friendship and hostility. The "friends," or the community, gravitate toward the pole of friendship; the "enemies," be they individuals, groups, or states, center around the pole of hostility. In-between are the indifferent groups or states— that is, those that are neither particularly friendly nor particularly hostile, but among which can be found groups or states cooperating on an *ad hoc*, temporary basis.

All groups bearing upon the formation of foreign policy, including all states that are members of the international society, can thus be placed in one of three classifications:

the community, the enemies, and the indifferent groups or states from among which temporary collaborators might be recruited. The community has been defined as the group formed as the result of "community-building" objectives in the past, and whose interests are taken into account in foreign policy. Since "enemies" do not belong to the community, they must be the result of past failure to build up or enlarge the community; they are those whose interests are not satisfied through a particular foreign policy. Groups or states that cooperate with policy-makers on an *ad hoc* basis can be defined as those that were not implicated in past policy but whose interests are being satisfied by current policy. Their relationship might be called one of temporary collaboration or accommodation of interests. Temporary collaborators may, of course, in time become members of the community or else enemies.

We may take it for granted that the acquisition of enemies does not just happen. They must be traceable to some past actions of the ego-state and/or alter-states, and they are, in fact, traceable to failure to respect and satisfy the interests of states or groups in the past. Enemies are the consequence of past failure to implement wishes or demands presented to policy-makers; alternatively, enemies are the result of jeopardizing certain interests in order to satisfy other demands. A state has enemies not only because its policies have in the past ignored or harmed the interests of other states or groups—for instance, by aggression—but also because it may have refused to yield to certain demands—as, for example, Turkey refused Soviet demands in respect of the Straits, or as the French Government has in the past ignored the demands of the French Communist Party for a pro-Soviet policy. No policy-maker can, of course, satisfy all the demands made on him, nor can he, even if he wanted to, avoid infringing upon some interest or other. But, in making their choices, policy-makers cannot disregard some interests and favor others just as they please. By satisfying some interests, they help to fortify their community; by ignoring or overriding others, they create enemies. In the context of the study of aims of foreign policy, enemies may therefore be defined as "results of past disregard of interests." Foreign policy may be viewed not only as a process through which communities grow and decay, but also as a process through which enemies are made and unmade.

These considerations are the reasons why both communities and enemies can be conceived of as the results of past foreign policies. What is more, communities and enemies also project their influence on the future. Communities hold together and grow only if they are fostered and cultivated. Communities continuously shed some of their members and they require a steady supply of new recruits. Through their foreign policy, policy-makers therefore need to recruit new supporters and to strengthen and consolidate the ties that bind existing members. Policy-makers are the builders of community.

Even more pervasive, perhaps, are the consequences of having enemies, of past disregard of interests. Enemies do not forget, and in their policies they will seek to reassert their interests. The price of disregard of interests is reduced freedom of action, the need for vigilance, and the need to guard against hostile designs. All states take steps to maintain their policies against the opposition of their enemies; a part of their foreign-policy operations is devoted to keeping enemies at bay.

In keeping with these definitions, we can distinguish three types of interests: (1) demands of the community (demands that are the result of past objectives); (2) demands of temporary collaborators (demands that relate to current objectives, but that are not the result of past objectives); and (3) demands of enemies (demands, or interests, that are disregarded at the expense of future objectives).

Earlier in this book, power-input was classified according to whether it was attributable to power-resources, to current power-output, or to liabilities (future power-output). In the same way we can now distinguish between interests due to past objectives and those that result in current and future objectives. The demands of enemies cannot, strictly speaking, be considered as interests in the usual meaning of the word, because their distinguishing characteristic is the fact that they are disregarded. On similar grounds, power-input obtained as the result of incurring liabilities cannot be described as a true increment to power, because it involves a future drain on power. But in formulating interests, the policy-maker considers all the demands made with regard to his policy. He may choose to disregard some of the expressions of interest, but he cannot ignore the effect of this disregard on his own future policies.

The distinction between internal and external interests corresponds to that between internal and external power-input. Internal interests are the wishes and requests, in respect to the behavior of other states, made by groups and individuals residing in the policy-makers' own state. External interests are those expressed by policy-makers of other states and by groups and individuals within them. This distinction is based on the origin of the wish or desire and on the differences in the mode of expression and communication of these two kinds of demand.

The concept of "interests" put forward in this study is not to be confused with that of "national interest." The phrase "national interest" has been avoided in this discussion; it is not a term that can be defined with clarity. Few deny today that foreign policy ought not to be conducted in disregard of the national interest, but there is difficulty in securing general agreement upon the substantive meaning of the concept. Assent to the general proposition does not remove the difficulties of securing agreement on what specific definition of national interest is to be adopted in each particular case. The "nation" itself is a concept that defies exact definition. The proposition that policy-makers pursue, or should pursue,

the national interest is therefore singularly unenlightening.
"National interest" postulates the existence of only one
type of community whose demands policy-makers must obey
—that is, the nation, defined presumably as all the citizens of
a state. And yet policy-makers have been known to accede
to the demands of groups smaller than the nation, or larger
than the nation and not belonging to it (such as other states).
There is nothing out of the ordinary, or traitorous, in policy-
makers paying heed to subnational, other-national, or supra-
national interests. Policies are often advocated as being "in
the national interests," but they are always advocated by
groups or individuals or other states, never by the "nation."
By referring to the national interest, the individuals, groups,
or associations advocating a policy assert that this policy is
also in the interest of others. Strictly speaking, however, no
one can claim to act as spokesman for the nation and its
interests, except perhaps the policy-maker.

The view that foreign policy aims at the attainment of
national interests has important theoretical consequences. The
national interest is a static concept that may partially and
in a vague way explain why policy is what it is, but it is of
little avail in the dynamic analysis of foreign policy in which
changes in foreign policy have to be examined. It postulates
that policy-makers are responsible to only one type of community—the nation—and therefore excludes the possibility
of changes in the composition of the policy-maker's community. As we have tried to show, the community is not
immutable; it changes in accordance with the kind of policy
pursued by governments. Those who use the "national-inter-
est" concept can account for changes in foreign policy in only
one of two ways: either by assuming the national interest to
remain constant and explaining changes as the result of other
factors (such as power or the policy of other states); or else
by attributing those changes to variations in the policy-
maker's or the nation's *views* of what the best national inter-

est is. With its emotional overtones of perennial and majestic dignity, the national interest is unsuitable as a concept for the analysis of those "turbulent streams of human desires and predispositions that somehow merge in the decisions of those who make foreign policies."[8]

There is a sense in which national interest connotes the primary, basic claim on the loyalty of policy-makers by reference to which other demands should be evaluated. It might be argued that the interests of allies, for instance, should be taken into account only because doing so will increase the national power, whereas the interests of the nation deserve automatic protection in their own right. But the policy-makers' primary loyalties may belong to a group smaller than the nation—as, for example, in France, where, in the 1950's, foreign policy was conducted with the support of barely two thirds of the population. Alternatively, basic loyalty is due to a dominating foreign power, as happens in the case of satellite or semicolonial governments. Since the concept of national interest does not explain all the interests a government has to bear in mind, we cannot accede to the view that foreign policy seeks to satisfy the national interest. Just as the sources of the power of a state are found both within and beyond the confines of the nation, so the interests defended by the policy-makers are those of groups that are only part of the nation or else outside it. A theory of foreign policy cannot determine in advance of empirical investigation whose interests are furthered by the foreign policy of a given government; it can merely say that the interests will belong to a number of groups found both within and outside the state.

Internal and External Interests

The influence of the foreign-policy organizations (the armed forces, the diplomatic services, and the administration)

[8] Frederick S. Dunn, *War and the Minds of Men* (New York: Harper & Brothers, 1950), p. 17.

is widely recognized. Disposing of internal channels of communication, their members have the best facilities for bringing their views to the attention of policy-making bodies through explicit recommendations or through situation reports suggestive of definite policies. As executors of foreign policy, they are in close touch with the practical side of action and are intensely interested in the most efficient implementation of agreed policies. They dislike internal and external interference with national power-resources and view with favor increases in their power-input. Foreign-policy organizations, too, as a rule enjoy a special position in their society. We would therefore expect their members to work for the preservation of their status and to combat external threats to their position in particular (for instance, those arising from defeat, subjection, or lack of success in military or diplomatic contests). They naturally incline toward courses of action that help to enhance their own importance to the public. They resent public criticism of foreign policies as amateurish and misinformed interference in matters within their particular competence.

Contrasting with the tightly knit foreign-policy organizations is the internal community at large. All citizens are potentially, but not actually, its members. In an internally tranquil state there may not be much difference between the citizen body and the policy-maker's internal community. In some other states, such as France, the internal community is at times significantly smaller. But no matter whether we analyze a stable society or a state rent by civil strife, the policy-maker's community and the internal backing on which he can count depend on the policy he pursues.

Diffuse collectivities, such as the internal community, cannot easily voice their interests. That function is performed by parties and by interest groups; the wishes of single citizens count for little unless they are taken up by one of these political associations and thereby reconciled with other similar and, sometimes, conflicting individual demands. Such preliminary coordination of interests of individuals and of small groups is an important function of the more inclusive political groups.

Political parties are the most important multipurpose links between the policy-makers and individual, specific, and local interests. Their importance for the study of foreign policy lies in the fact that, generally speaking, they are nationwide in scope and reflect a variety of interests. The bigger the parties, and the fewer parties there are, the more interests they represent, and the greater the difficulties they face in the task of reconciling and coordinating such a variety of interests. Representing clusters of interests, parties can adopt authoritative and consistent attitudes on the whole range of foreign-policy problems confronting the state. But that same breadth of outlook required of them on the large issues makes them liable to lose touch with the multitude of particular interests on whose satisfaction their vitality depends. In addition to voicing and satisfying the interests of those whom they represent, parties also defend the interests of their own organizations, and these organizational interests become relevant to foreign policy whenever they are endangered, or are capable of being promoted, by the actions of other states.

The activities of political parties do not render superfluous the other associations, permanent or transitory, that make it their task to influence the government on a variety of specific issues, including those of foreign policy, and that, following political-science usage, may be called "interest groups." The type and composition of interest groups vary with the social structure of the country; but modern countries have evolved forms through which business and managerial elements, organized labor, the churches, the farmers and the peasants, national racial or cultural minorities, and veterans' groups— as well as regional, provincial, and local interest groups—can give expression to their interests. Every country also has smaller groups concerned exclusively with international affairs and with relations with foreign countries, such as foreign trade and investment organizations, overseas transport and communications concerns, international friendship and cultural societies, United Nations associations, pacifist movements, etc. An important role in giving shape to, and reflecting and representing, many of the most important interests is also played by the government administration. Most governments have one or more departments, such as ministries for industry, trade, or commerce, that maintain contact with the country's industrial and trading world, be it composed of private or nationalized concerns. The department of labor is usually in close touch with the unions, while the ministry of agriculture, not unnaturally, develops a considerable understanding of the wishes of farmers and peasants. Through such "vertical" connections, interest groups have an opportunity to voice their views at various stages of the policy-making process—for instance, in interdepartmental consultations or in the process of policy execution.

Like all other claimants, political parties and interest groups are concerned with changing the behavior of other states by inducing the policy-makers to take up their causes and implement them through foreign-policy operations. They may desire protection from hostile activities of "foreigners," or they may want their own government to induce other governments to act in a manner favorable to their interests. Protection may be requested by nationals who reside and work outside their country of origin. Groups within a country may ask for protection from such actions of other states as tariffs or immigration restrictions, or they may request special defense measures for exposed or outlying areas, such as Hong Kong.

Apart from expressing special and particular interests, the political associations also seek to influence all other foreign-policy operations and, through them, the policies of other states. Each single foreign-policy adjustment affects all the other foreign-policy operations of the government and, therefore, also those operations in which the given political group is especially interested. Every measure can be amended or adjusted in such a way as to change the incidence of rewards or sacrifices that are consequent upon its execution; for instance, various attempts were made to amend the U.S. Economic Cooperation Act of 1948 with a view to meeting the demands of special interest groups, and the shipping interests in particular succeeded in obtaining the provision that 50 per cent of all sea-borne goods financed out of ECA funds should be carried by American ships.

Consideration of the exclusive goals of special interests should not obscure the extent to which interests may overlap and coalesce on the basis of an agreed formula. Some interests, such as the threat of foreign invasion, are capable of rallying near-universal support. On other issues, the homogeneity of parties, interest groups, and also of members of foreign-policy organizations may be confined to one issue and to one interest only. Thus, French opposition to German rearmament may unite Communists, Gaullists, neutralists, anti-Germans, army circles, etc.; in other words, groups that would refuse to cooperate on other issues. The present survey serves to identify some of the components of which the interest alignment on any side issue may be formed within the policy-makers' internal community.

The policy-makers' external community comprises two main categories: policy-makers of friendly states, and individuals and groups in other states.

First and foremost in importance as members of the external community are the policy-makers of friendly states. The closest association prevails among those states that, as the result of some previous common political experience, regard themselves as members of one great family. The British Commonwealth and the relations between the Scandinavian states are examples of contacts that have been intimate and friendly as a matter of course for long periods. Friendly relations, too, sometimes arise between a great power and some of the smaller states situated within its orbit. Such are, or have been for a time, the relations between the United States and Latin American countries, between Britain and Belgium, Holland, or Portugal, or between Russia and Bulgaria. They may be formalized in an explicit commitment to defense from aggression, or they may be based on a long-standing tradition, the smaller states customarily following the lead of the great power in exchange for the latter's scrupulous regard for their rights. Third, we have the special relationship that exists between a dominant power and its satellites. As the direct appointees or even the nationals of the dominant power, satellite policy-makers find it difficult to continue in office without the support of the dominant power. Since in their policy they pay less attention to the interests of their internal community, they receive less support from inside their country, which in turn makes them less able to assert their independence toward the dominant power, should they desire to do so. The U.S.S.R.'s European satellites are examples of such states; protectorates and semicolonial regimes constitute a similar type. Last of all, there are the declared allies of a policy-maker. The friendship of allies is more intense and more productive of results than the other types of external community relationships, but the period within which alliances are fully effective is, as a rule, shorter. An alliance is not a commitment to common action on all issues; but the logic of cooperation frequently extends the range of common policies and the scope of common interests beyond the narrower limits set in formal documents. The interests of the external community are the wishes of allied and friendly states. Friendly policy-makers may be interested in securing support for their policies toward a third state, in obtaining contributions to their own power-input, and in minimizing actions that they consider unfriendly or injurious. Making and sustaining a multitude of such demands is the daily bread of diplomatic intercourse.

The other important elements in the policy-makers' external community are individuals and groups in other states.[9] The policy-makers' internal community does not always comprise all those formally subject to their authority. Political groups whose interests thus remain unsatisfied tend to look for satisfaction to other states, becoming members of the external community or temporary collaborators of other states.

National minorities are among the more important nongovernmental members of the external community. Minorities are formed all over the world; they arise whenever a group—whether ethnic, racial, or linguistic—is more conscious of its bonds with another state than with the community among which it lives. The quality of minority organizations and the urgency of the minority interests are sometimes less the result of the intensity of the grievances they harbor than of the expansionist aims and power of their countries of origin. Their interests may be conveyed directly to the policy-makers, or else they may be channeled through political groups in their mother countries—parties, nationalist organizations—that make it their special business to look after the interests of their compatriots in other countries. National minorities may be interested in action aimed at bringing about a change in the policy of their adopted country, and their demands may range from requests for minor protective measures to demands for direct intervention and outright annexation. Or else they may seek to maintain their separate identity by requesting funds or ways of preserving contacts with their mother country.

[9] The criterion of nationality or citizenship is a convenient one for distinguishing between members of the internal community and the policy-makers' external community. All non-nationals whose wishes are taken into account in foreign policy, such as members of national minorities abroad, belong to the external community; nationals residing abroad, on the other hand, may be regarded as part of the internal community.

Ideological and spiritual followers abroad may also be counted among the external community. Communist Party members and sympathizers in non-Communist countries are obvious examples of ideological supporters. Nazi and fascist supporters before and during World War II, supporters of *Peronismo* in South America, members of the Moslem Brotherhood in the Middle East, and even the democratic socialist parties of Europe and Asia are other instances of the same phenomenon. The supreme interest of ideological groups lies in the conquest of power; they wish their ideological fatherland to abstain from actions that would delay that event and seek positive assistance toward their goal.

National and seminational organizations with branches abroad represent borderline cases between the internal and external communities. These may be private business concerns operating in foreign countries, such as the American oil companies in the Middle East; or they may be partly or entirely state-owned industrial, transport, and trade corporations. Various other organizations of a nonbusiness character fall within this category: schools, universities, and cultural institutes abroad, churches, missionary societies, expert advisory teams, and the like. They all seek the protection and the assistance of the home government. They usually are in a good position to advance their interests either through their local diplomatic representative or through their connections with interest groups in their home state.

Relations between the policy-maker and his community have a relative permanence, or at least persistence. Policy-makers are expected to defend the interests of all the members of their community. But the policy-maker also enjoys the benefit of supporters whose collaboration is of a more temporary and a more limited character and is the product of deals, bargains, and fleeting alignments. The division between the more permanent and the more temporary alignments is not a sharp one, but it is sufficiently distinct to justify separate discussions of problems associated with temporary collaboration. Parties to a deal are expected to adhere to the terms of that agreement, but they are not expected to take into account other interests of their partners not relevant to it.

Temporary collaboration is a phenomenon of the twilight zone between enmity and friendship, between the community and its enemies. Temporary collaborators wear, as it were, two hats: They are potential members of the community, whose interests are therefore entitled to careful consideration; but they may also be future enemies or may have been enemies in the past, and should therefore be treated with caution. Temporary collaboration may thus assume the appearance either of friendly cooperation or of a grudging accommodation of interests.

Just as the extent of the external community is comparatively narrower than that of the internal community, so the scope of temporary cooperation and accommodation of interests is wider in the international than in the domestic field. Most states of the world are capable of cooperating with each other on a temporary basis, whereas they would not all be eligible to join in the external community. Diplomacy operates on the basis of the formal presumption that all states are friendly and acceptable bargaining partners. The permanent diplomatic contact in which policy-makers remain with most states provides the machinery by which all manner of deals can conveniently be arranged. International organizations, too, are meeting grounds for those wishing to enter into limited forms of cooperation. Voting in the U.N. General Assembly often provides a good example of combined action on narrow issues. In all such dealings, policy-makers assume the obligation to take account of other states' interests in certain specified matters—for instance, by joining them in a diplomatic démarche, or in certain commercial matters, in exchange for support or concessions on other specified occasions.

Among the external political groups from which temporary collaborators are recruited, the following might be mentioned: collaborationists, exiled persons, opposition parties and groups, and alienized groups. Collaborationists are the supporters of an alien occupying power in an occupied country. Conditions of collaboration arise in wartime and in a postwar period, but they can also be observed in colonial and other areas where the legitimacy of the ruling power is not generally recognized. Since administration of an occupied country requires at least a modicum of cooperation with its inhabitants, the occupying power cannot wholly disregard the interests of the local population. Collaborationists express some of these interests, but their lot is a difficult one; despised by their compatriots and by the occupying power alike, their wishes cannot carry much weight. Equally weak is the position of emigrés, and yet their demands cannot be altogether ignored. Political refugees tend to forgather in countries opposed to regimes of their homelands and become spokesmen for their countries' interests in the host-state. Sometimes they are the collaborationists of the future. They may also fill advisory and expert positions in foreign-policy organizations and succeed in influencing the formation of policy toward their country.

Cooperation with foreign opposition parties (as distinct from ideological followers firmly committed to one particular power) is even more tenuous and transitory than with collaborationists and emigrés. In democratic regimes, opposition parties are so much part and parcel of the ruling political system that they are loath to invoke foreign support. In totalitarian regimes, opposition itself is tantamount to treason and contact with foreign groups, to espionage and subversion. There are, however, occasions on which opposition parties invoke external assistance or ask policy-makers to adopt certain policies or abstain from others. We can mention in this connection British and United States efforts to aid opposition parties in Eastern Europe after 1945, and the anti-Mossadegh forces in Iran in 1953.

Finally, we come to the interests of alienized groups, which clamor for aid and support from the policy-makers of other states. Alienized groups can be described as groups that find it difficult to adjust themselves to the framework of the state in which they live; rather than change the policies of that state, these groups would set up their own autonomous territorial unit. Unlike minority groups, they are not interested in linking themselves with another state, and they do not claim support on grounds of national loyalty. They seek to establish their own state, and in this enterprise they need foreign assistance. At any given moment throughout the world, there are several regions where such potential new states are in the process of emerging: in colonial and semidependent areas, in "backward" territories or otherwise nationally oppressed regions. All policy-makers must adopt an attitude toward such groups, and some of them may find it expedient to espouse their cause. The backing they offer may range from support at international meetings or conferences and individual remonstrations to the "oppressor" to attempts to sway world opinion, and ultimately to passive or active support in an eventual resistance campaign or civil war.

Such are, in outline, the external groups with which policy-makers may temporarily cooperate. In an ideal international society, the interests of all inhabitants of a state would be perfectly expressed by their own government. But in an imperfect world, some internal political organizations seek the support of governments other than their own, and frequently get it. Such support, when granted, is fraught with dangers, frequently borders on subversion, and is not conducive to international understanding and friendly intercourse; but it is requested precisely under conditions that fall short of friendly intercourse.

Although greater importance must be assigned to temporary

collaboration in the external field, mention must be made of the interests arising from internal temporary collaboration. States ruled by coalition governments present many examples of this form of cooperation between the policy-makers and various political parties. But the same phenomenon can be observed in all states, wherever political groups or individuals not belonging to the policy-makers' community succeed in cooperating with the policy-makers on a narrow issue or for the fulfillment of a transient interest. In moments of external danger—e.g., foreign aggression—policy-makers may obtain the temporary support of groups otherwise bitterly opposed to them; but, more often than not, it is the limited, calculated collaboration obtained by specified concessions and compromises that we have in mind when speaking of internal temporary collaboration.

"Enemies," as a concept, admits of gradations; there are differences among competitors, rivals, opponents, and bitter enemies. A state has few, if any, enemies with whom it is ready to fight to the bitter end; but it may have rivals and competitors whose interests it cannot satisfy, and others who for some reason or other are dissatisfied with its policies. The interests of enemies are interests that, although expressed to policy-makers (for instance, through protest notes), are ignored or violated by their foreign policy. No foreign policy can satisfy all interests and no policy-maker can avoid having enemies. But in addition to having to contend with this inescapable dilemma of policy, the policy-maker may be led to ignore certain interests because by doing so he simplifies policy-making. He may be able to save time that would otherwise be consumed in lengthy consultations and protracted negotiations with the affected parties. But the immediate advantage of making policy by disregarding interests is counterbalanced by the dissatisfaction and hostility created by such behavior. For policy-makers, the principal reason for taking such interests into consideration, rather than ignoring or injuring them, is to forestall an adverse reaction by states affected by their policy. In 1950, the North Koreans evidently failed to foresee the reaction of the United States and the United Nations.

Policy-makers have both external and internal enemies. Internal enemies are those groups and individuals whose interests are disregarded and who are dissatisfied with and oppose the foreign policy of their country. Political groups belonging to the external community of a policy-maker (minorities or ideological followers) are the "enemies" of the state in which they are located. Not all the opponents of the policy-makers' activities are determined to establish and maintain relations with foreign-policy–makers; some of them are merely dissatisfied and refuse to support the current policy of their country.

We will conclude this survey of interests with a brief discussion of the policy-makers' own specific interests.

The tasks and functions of policy-makers have already been examined at some length. We shall now limit ourselves to showing how foreign states may affect the performance of these tasks and therefore become the immediate object of concern. Policy-makers resent interference by other states in the relations between themselves and their community, and they oppose attempts at weakening their links with their community in the fields of "formulation of interests" and of "procurement of power-input." Policy-makers seek to augment and reinsure their power-input and oppose hostile actions aimed at reducing it, because power-input is indispensable for implementing their tasks; in this sense alone can power be an aim of foreign policy. They reject interference with their foreign-policy organizations and seek to reduce the obstacles to an efficient execution of policy. The policy-makers' interests lie in minimizing interference and maximizing friendly cooperation in the implementation of the foreign-policy functions.

A second group of interests arises out of the policy-makers' role as guardians of the interests of the community; this invariably comes to mean the guardians of all the interests of the community, which comprise the interests of the entire community. The foreign policy of a country does not exist solely in order to satisfy the explicit wishes and desires of the people. Policy-makers are a great deal more than just a rubber stamp for popular preferences and policies. They hold their own views about foreign policy, they contribute some power-input to foreign policy, they play an influential role in the formation of general policy and in the coordination of interests in particular. They even claim to know what is "good for the people." For these reasons, policy-makers can be considered as a separate group, exercising an influence on foreign policy akin to that of other interest groups.

In the realm of power, policy-makers seek to ensure the efficient transformation of power-input into power-output; in the realm of aims, their concern is with the translation of interests into objectives of foreign policy. Policy-makers are the recipients of all claims that members of their community choose to advance with regard to foreign policy, but they cannot translate all of them into foreign-policy operations in the exact form in which they are presented. Students of politics are familiar with the proposition that there is "a gap between the notion of what may be called the general or common interest of a community . . . and the joint or several interests of its members considered as separate people. The former is not the sum of the latter and may be extremely different from it."[10] In foreign policy, the general interest is not the sum total of the separate interests of all the members of the community, because these interests are not all compatible with each other. The satisfaction of some of them prevents the implementation of others. The general interest is the coordinated interest of the members of the community. Policy-makers achieve this coordination, which is a precondition for

[10] T. D. Weldon, *States and Morals: A Study in Political Conflicts* (London: John Murray, 1946), p. 37.

the defining of objectives, by inducing some members of the community to sacrifice some of their interests in order to make possible the fulfillment of others of their own interests and some of the interests of other members of the community. They may accommodate new interests by associating them with traditional demands and by retaining their antecedents in national policy. The fewer groups or states they injure or offend in the process, the better. The greater the number of supporters they succeed in rallying behind an interest, the more successful their policy.

In the process of coordinating the interests of their community, policy-makers cannot ignore the rule that a certain minimum of interests belonging to all members of the community must at all costs be safeguarded. Failure to protect them will undermine the unity and cohesion of the community and reduce its membership. These minimum interests are those whose abandonment by the policy-makers sets in motion the processes of dissociation and creation of enemies. Every community cherishes certain interests above all else: These are its minimum interests. They are common to the entire community, being the lowest common denominator of its consensus; they are so important and so well grounded that they turn into "principles" and gain unquestionable and unreasoned acceptance. They become part of the articles of faith and are upheld with great vigor. Any important and general interest can be supported in this enduring and passionate manner. Frequently, the integrity of national territory or of political institutions can become the object of such attachment. It may be a cherished friendship, like the belief in the British Commonwealth, or the assertion of some claim to superiority or exclusive right, like "command of the seas" or the Monroe Doctrine. For the Communist policy-maker, loyalty to the U.S.S.R. constitutes one such irreducible and unquestioned principle of policy. The concept of "minimum interest" has no fixed content. This content is variable and embraces all interests that are generally and firmly upheld. But whatever the content, no policy-maker can ignore minimum interests when translating interests into objectives.

This extensive review of the input of interests was not intended as a description of the exact composition of the stream of interests confronting the policy-makers of any particular state. As in the case of power-input, the object was to indicate the main categories in terms of which interests can be classified and changes in interests accounted for. With the help of the concepts of "community," "enemies," and "temporary collaboration," it has also been possible to indicate the conceptual links between "interests" and "objectives." We may now turn to the analysis of objectives.

Objectives of Foreign Policy

Objectives are the aims of foreign-policy operations. They define the policy that it is desired to induce in other states and that is to be attained through foreign-policy operations. Foreign policy is concerned with the conduct of other states; it does not and cannot bring about conditions that are not consequent upon the behavior of one's own and other states. Hence the foreign-policy objectives of a state describe only the desired behavior of other states and, by implication, the expected and desirable change in behavior. The desired change in behavior implied in an objective is the difference between actual and desirable conduct. It is the difference between a state's present, actual foreign policy and its future, desirable foreign policy. Examples of objectives are: the passing of a resolution in the U.N. (inducing a majority of U.N. members to vote for it), the military defeat of a state, concessions in international negotiations, the maintenance of a friendly government. The statement that peace is the objective of a policy is meaningful, though admittedly vague: It means that this policy seeks to induce other states to abstain from warlike operations; it has no other meaning in the context of foreign-policy analysis. Thus, all objectives are definitions of conduct that it is deemed desirable to establish or to maintain in another state or in a number of other states. By consciously defining objectives in terms of the desired policy of other states, we throw into relief the magnitude of the difference between the desired and the actual policy and therefore give an indication of the size of effort required to bring about the desired change.

Objectives indicate the actions that other states are to perform and also the tasks required of foreign-policy organizations of the "ego" state. Here is a quotation from the instructions given to the commander of the Allied force about to make a landing in Norway in 1940: "His Majesty's Government and the Government of the French Republic have decided to land an expedition in Central Norway with the object of: (a) providing encouragement for the Norwegian Government, (b) forming a rallying point for the Norwegian Government and armed forces, (c) securing a base for any subsequent operations in Scandinavia. . . ." The parts of the instructions relating to the Norwegian Government are those that explicitly state the actions of other states that it is desirable to attain. The position of the Norwegian Government is to be strengthened by Allied support and its armed forces are to be reinforced. It is furthermore implied that the Norwegian Government will not offer resistance to the Allied landing force and to the establishment of a base for further operations in Scandinavia. In addition, the instructions imply a certain course of action on the part of the German troops that the Allied force is to bring about: A landing can be effected and a base secured only if German counteractions are frustrated by the Allied force. In this way, the instructions, a typical definition of objectives, combine a partly implicit description of the desired conduct of alter-states with an equally partly explicit formulation of the tasks of the foreign-policy organizations of the ego-state.

To formulate the desirable policy of other states and set the tasks of foreign-policy organizations in relation to it are among the chief tasks of policy-makers. Orders and instructions to their own organizations and claims, protests, and requests to other states are the main methods by which they acquit themselves of their responsibility. They issue instructions to diplomatic missions and to delegates at international conferences and set the terms that negotiators seek to realize in their talks with foreign representatives. Army commanders receive orders about the movements and tasks of their units, just as the heads of the propaganda, intelligence, and other services are given directives about their respective spheres of activity. Other sectors of the country's administrative machinery may also be requested to undertake, or to stop, actions affecting the policies of other states. On the other hand, policy-makers address requests and protests to the governments of other states and specify in them the course of action that should be pursued or indicate the behavior to which objections are raised. Such requests or protests may also announce the type of action that the ego-state may undertake in this connection: A diplomatic protest or ultimatum may detail or imply the steps that will be taken if certain specific requests are not heeded; a request for support or for other favorable action may mention the *quid pro quo* offered.

It is axiomatic that every foreign-policy operation has an objective. Without one, an operation is merely a waste of effort, unrelated to any foreign-policy function. Objectives are the elements of foreign policy that fit every operation into the wider pattern of the strategy of statecraft. Just as the notion of the necessity of power-input suggests a theoretical approach picturing the foreign-policy operations of a state from the point of view of power, so the axiom of the necessity of objectives provides the theoretical completion of that picture. An *ex post* account of the objectives associated with each power-output can give a full outline of the foreign-policy operations of a state. The listing of power-outputs—"visible" or "tangible" evidence of the existence of foreign-policy operations—is the first step in this accounting of foreign policy. The determination of the objectives associated with each operation would be the second, though more difficult, step in such an attempt. A forward-looking strategy of foreign policy would similarly begin by laying down the framework of objectives within which foreign policy is going to be executed.

It is by no means easy to determine all the objectives of a foreign policy over a given period. Policy is seldom clearly formulated—even basic policy. Most policies are carried out on a routine basis. Indeed, they must be, for a policy-maker who wished constantly to define and redefine all his objectives would not have any time left for his other duties. The need for a formulation of objectives arises only in cases of changes in policy, including changes in objectives. The reformulation of objectives should take place simultaneously with the discussion or execution of policy changes. This is by no means an impossible task. Objectives are most often explicitly formulated when changes in policy are being made.

While certain objectives are explicit, others may remain implicit. Some routine operations have implicit objectives that need never be asserted or openly pursued. Thus, the general tasks and routine duties of foreign-policy organizations are not subject to doubt: The army protects the frontiers of the state, the coast guard keeps the coast secure, the diplomat represents his country and argues its case. Nor need these organizations be instructed by policy-makers in the details of their duties or their internal routine arrangements. But policy-makers will have to set the sights wherever a change in policy is contemplated. The army must be told to give special protection to frontier A, the coast guard to be on the lookout for vessel B, and the diplomat to present a well-argued case at meeting C.

Like interests, objectives are closely linked with the concepts of "community" and "enemies." The community was earlier defined as the result of past objectives; it follows, therefore, that the community can be created and maintained through the pursuit of objectives, too. The question arises: What are the "community-building" objectives? Enemies are groups or states whose interests were disregarded or harmed in the past. A second question arises: What are the consequences of having enemies? What proportion of foreign-policy operations is to be devoted to defensive operations against such enemies? Finally, one may ask: How much more can a state do after it has taken care of its "community-building" and defensive commitments? Let us examine each question in turn.

In what sense can we speak of objectives creating and maintaining a community? Communities are what the policy-makers make of them. If policy-makers pursue objectives that reflect the interests of a large number of groups and states, their community will flourish and expand. If they pursue objectives that offend many groups and states, or even harm their interests, the community will decline and contract. Thus policy-makers will (a) pursue or abandon certain objectives in order to strengthen their community, and (b) adapt other objectives so as to minimize the harm and maximize the advantage they may entail in regard to its cohesion. For example, the abandonment by France of its claims of rights in Egypt and the Sudan was motivated by a desire to achieve the Entente Cordiale in 1904.

Community-building takes two main forms: (1) consolidation of the existing community, and (2) the recruitment of new members.

Policy-makers resort to a variety of means in order to maintain the cohesion of the community. Certain of their operations have the sole purpose of retaining their supporters— notably, many actions of the ceremonial and symbolic kind, such as the exchange of visits, maintenance of close contact, consultations, friendly gestures toward members of the community, participation in a common ritual. In all their operations, policy-makers seek to avoid offending their supporters; they avoid expressions of hostility toward them, they emphasize the things that the community has in common, and minimize the differences dividing it. Of course, not all policy-makers will conduct their policy so as to offend none of their supporters; certain objectives may be so important that policy-makers may push forward with them at the risk of damaging the unity of the community. On the other hand, each time a policy-maker succeeds in satisfying an interest, he has also succeeded in strengthening his community.

The recruitment of new members is an important preoccupation of policy-makers. The adoption or abandonment of certain objectives in order to acquire wider support at home is not an infrequent political event. The search for new allies animates many diplomatic moves. Gestures of real or pretended magnanimity, such as the Soviet renunciation of reparation claims shortly before a German election, or acts of friendship, such as the granting of aid in an emergency situation, tend to increase the circle of one's friends. Finally, international relations offer a large number of situations, such as confrontation by a common danger, in which cooperation between states can be arranged by some adjustment of objectives.

Enemies are another source of concern to the policy-makers. Whereas the community-building part of their activities is directed toward the continuation of the community in the future, defensive activities aimed at neutralizing the enemy are essentially based on the past. A state that has successfully, but at great cost, repulsed an armed attack by another state may congratulate itself on having escaped the fate of subjection, but it may have little positive gain to show as the result. In this sense, defensive objectives do not contribute to satisfying the positive, forward-looking purposes of a community. The same considerations apply to domestic enemies; they severely restrict the freedom of action of policy-makers in the sphere of foreign policy.

In applying themselves to the pursuit of defensive and community-building objectives, policy-makers do not lose sight of immediate and positive objectives. Examples of such objectives include making the nation's views and requirements known abroad, tendering advice to one state, protesting to another, taking the initiative in the organization of international institutions or alliances, enlarging the nation's sphere of influence and power. All these international moves can be said to have positive objectives, whose implementation brings immediate gain, in contrast to defensive objectives, whose realization merely averts the hostile designs of an enemy, and to community-building objectives, whose fulfillment secures the future solidity of the community but in no way contributes to the satisfaction of its present interests.

We have noted the dualism in the definition of objectives that refers both to the desirable conduct of other states and to the foreign-policy operations of the ego-state aimed at bringing about this desirable conduct. This nexus between ego- and alter-state conduct is a crucial point in the definition of objectives. To choose the foreign-policy operation that will bring about the desired change in the policies of the other state is no mean task. Policy-makers may choose one of four basic methods of influencing other states—influencing their interests, their power-input, their objectives, or their power-output. For each of these methods, there is a corresponding defensive method of neutralizing it. We may thus classify objectives according to which of the "offensive" or "defensive" methods of influencing other states they employ. Methods of inducing changes in the foreign policy of other states will be discussed in Part IV.

Aims and Principles

No student of foreign policy can evade adopting an attitude toward principles of foreign policy, a topic that looms large in the literature of international relations. We have noted in Part I that "norms" or "principles"—that is, sentiments that certain foreign-policy actions are desirable in themselves—are among the elements of foreign policy. We must now discuss the relation of principles to the aims of foreign policy and to policy in general.

We may distinguish two types of foreign-policy principles: those that are conveyed by the community to the policy-makers along with interests, and those that guide or limit foreign-policy objectives. The "principled interests" assert the necessity of performing an action by virtue of its inherent justice or righteousness or of abstaining from other policies because of their inherent wickedness. Examples of such interests are advocacy of foreign aid on grounds of humanitarianism, or opposition to a policy because it is described as aggression. "Principled objectives" are pursued because of a belief in their unconditional validity. Action in accordance with international law, strict adherence to treaties and agreements, and respect for the recommendations of international institutions are instances of this type of principle. Since both types are in some respects identical with interests and objectives, we are able to subsume their discussion under that of aims of foreign policy.

Principles are inextricably fused with aims of foreign policy. A change in aims leads to a change in principles. A principle such as "noninterference in domestic affairs" or "free trade" is proclaimed and advocated when a state finds advantage in doing so. This close link between principles and aims of foreign policy is recognized by, and is one of the main tenets of, the "realist" writers in the field of international relations.

Some of them conclude that principles are a mere sham, a hypocritical cloak for selfish designs.

The prevalence and persistent resort to principles in the conduct of state affairs would suggest, however, that they perform an important function in the efficient pursuit of foreign policy. The usefulness of principles derives from their simplicity, forcefulness, and generality. Aims impel action by virtue of the beneficial consequences expected to follow from it. Principles are commands to act inspired by a strong sentiment that such action is worth doing for its own sake. Further, while aims are usually concrete and particular, principles are general and abstract, applicable to a variety of cases. Finally, principles are characterized by the simplicity of their formulation. In these three respects, foreign-policy principles are distinguishable from foreign-policy aims.

Principles are simple guides to action. Contrasted with the complexities of the decision-making process, they provide simple solutions of sloganlike clarity. The simpler they are, the more persuasive and, within limits, the more useful they can be. Confronted with an unending stream of choices, policy-makers have to rely on a number of standardized, ready-made solutions, transmitted to them as the distilled wisdom of experience or as the accepted precepts of morality and law. The simplicity of principles is an important factor in facilitating both explanation and advocacy of policy and the communication of ideas between the policy-makers, their community, their foreign-policy organizations, and other states.

Principles are strong and they endure because they are held to be inherently righteous. Aims shift as soon as changing conditions alter the balance of advantage; principles change much more slowly because whoever holds them holds them firmly, without much reference to external events. Shared by policy-makers and the community, principles provide a sound basis on which agreed and stable policies can be formulated. Policy-makers who anchor their policies in accepted principles

enhance the community's confidence in these policies and secure a firm backing for them. Adherence to principles adds to
the self-confidence of both the policy-makers and their supporters, for it reduces doubt, avoids constant self-questioning,
and favors the pursuit of a consistent course of action. The
knowledge that a state adheres to certain principles makes the
behavior of that state more predictable for other states; it
makes expectations more reliable and adjustments to its policy
easier. The strength and endurance of principles smoothe and
stabilize relations, because relationships based on pure calculation of advantage can never be as stable and enduring as
those founded on advantage fortified by adherence to common
principles. In most instances of international cooperation, giving is not always equal to taking, and mutual advantage is not
always obvious. With the help of the principles, for example,
of generosity or charity, and given the value attached to honor-
ing agreements, such potential obstacles to cooperation are
partially overcome.

The third source of usefulness of principles is their generality. The utopians have been criticized for expressing the
preoccupations of particular states in the guise of universal
moral principles. Valid though it is, such criticism tends to
overlook the function of principles. Their generality or universality enables them to function as a bridge between various
particular aims. For cooperation to ensue, it is often necessary
to find a "formula" that, if it is to encompass the aims of
various groups or states, must be more general than any one
of them. In relations between the policy-makers and their
supporters, such principles are not seldom the platform on
which they can unite several groups in support of a common
policy; in the absence of common principles, such consensus
might be more difficult to achieve. In international negotiations, too, principles are resorted to for the purpose of registering whatever agreement can be reached; though much
derided for their small effectiveness, such formulas are often

better than no agreement at all. The generality of principles contributes to what Kennan has called the "unobtrusive, almost feminine, function of the gentle civilizer of national self-interest."[11] He attributes this role to the "concepts of international law and morality," but his observation applies equally to all principles of foreign policy that can be shared with other states. If the support of other states is to be gained for national policies, at least some of the national aspirations must be stated in universal terms—that is, in terms of principles upheld by other states, too. Doing so softens some of the sharp edges of demands based solely on national interests; it helps to dress them in a decent cloak and prevents them from giving offense by reason of their selfish bluntness. The generality of principles has also a coordinating effect. Principles that are accepted as valid within the foreign-policy organization or the community have a unifying and coordinating effect on the activities of subunits and subgroups and reduce the need for special instructions in unforeseen circumstances.

The dysfunctional effects of principles spring from the same characteristics that have just been discussed: simplicity, strength, and generality. There are certain circumstances in which these characteristics obstruct the efficient pursuit of policy.

In the first place, the simplicity of principles ignores the very real complexity of international life and of foreign-policy problems. Excessive resort to principles in decision-making militates against the careful consideration of all foreseeable consequences of action, encourages superficiality in the advocacy and explanation of policy, and may be a disturbing factor in relations between policy-makers and the community.

The tenacity with which principles are held is another source of danger. Principles do not lend themselves to quick

---

[11] Kennan, *American Diplomacy, 1900–1950*, p. 54.

adjustment. They are acquired early in men's lives and they take a long time to become rooted in larger groups as standardized solutions to common problems. Success, force of precedent and the aura of tradition, and social disapproval of their violation all combine to give them great endurance. By the same token, however, principles introduce an element of rigidity into behavior at times when quickly changing world conditions require correspondingly rapid adjustment of policy —for instance, in times of war—and also, to the extent that elements of a foreign policy have to be adjusted to changes in its other elements and in the foreign policies of other states, excessive leaning on principles may actually be harmful. To the extent that rationality in the formation of foreign policy is greater than in personal or local affairs by reason of the importance of the issues at stake and the responsibility attaching to every action, and to the extent that the alternative courses of action are more thoroughly explored before a decision and policies are subject to more careful scrutiny and critical review, there is less need to rely on principles, which at best can only be a rough and ready guide to action.

The generality of principles encourages cooperation and blunts the sharpness of the narrowly conceived aims of foreign policy, but it also tends to separate them from their unavoidable connection with these very aims. The principles of foreign policy create enlightened interest out of purely self-centered interest, but they cannot run totally counter to interest. At times, the generality of principles makes them appear to compel action, or the adoption of moralistic or doctrinaire attitudes on issues that have only a tenuous relation to the wishes and desires of the community. The typical situations with which statesmen have to deal are "unique," or, rather, more highly differentiated than other social situations. They lend themselves less to a standardized treatment than to case-by-case solutions. For this reason, principles find a more limited application in foreign policy than in national societies, where the actions of millions are not only adjusted, but in a real sense guided and organized by them.

All these arguments are designed to show that the utility of principles of foreign policy is a strictly limited one—not that principles, which by their very nature are abstract and unconditional, exert no impact on foreign policy. Because of the close link between principles and aims of foreign policy, the impact that does occur can be analyzed in the same way as that of aims of foreign policy. If the wishes and desires conveyed to policy-makers contain expressions of principles, then for analytical purposes such principles do not differ from interests. If principles guide foreign-policy operations, they can be assimilated to objectives. To that extent, principles do not constitute one of the "variable" elements of foreign policy. They give rise to separate problems by reason of the features that distinguish them from aims—namely, simplicity, strength, and generality. Principles are a function of other aims of foreign policy (since all aims of foreign policy are interdependent), but changes in principles of foreign policy are slower than those in aims. They stabilize and slow down the working of adjustment processes. Their importance lies also in their generality, or even universality, in their ability to embody the common values and interests of many groups and states. For this reason, the analysis of principles plays an important part in studies of the conditions of stability of the international society (the system composed of interacting foreign policies), but is of no independent significance in the analysis of foreign policy.

PART FOUR

DYNAMICS OF FOREIGN POLICY

Determinants of Foreign Policy

The task of foreign-policy analysis, we may recall, is to throw light on the manner in which states influence each other. An essential preliminary of this task is to conceive of foreign policy, and describe it, as a process that is the resultant of a limited and determinate number of variable "elements" or "factors." The elements must be limited in number, or else the analysis of the interdependence of the variables would grow too complex; their number must be determinate, or else there would be no certainty that the analysis provides a complete answer to the problem we have set ourselves. But once foreign policy has been described in terms of such variables, the task of accounting for changes in foreign policy and of indicating the ways in which policy-makers seek to change the foreign policies of other states is relatively easy: Changes in foreign policy are defined as changes in one of the variable elements that make up foreign policy; the foreign policy of a state can be changed if one of the elements of that policy is altered.

In the preceding sections, foreign policy has been described as the resultant of four variable elements: power-input, power-output, interests, and objectives. The four elements were also assumed to be determined by the foreign policies of other states. Hence we can summarize the argument so far by saying that *the determinants of a foreign policy are: (1) its four elements—its power-input, power-output, interests, and objectives; and (2) the foreign policies of other states.*[12] This definition is the point of departure for the dynamic analysis of foreign policy; it lays down the framework within which answers to foreign-policy problems may be given. Acceptance of this way of conceiving of foreign policy depends on agreement with at least the outlines of the preceding argument. Once accepted, it opens up a fruitful approach to the study of problems of interaction and adjustment of foreign policies, for it has been devised for the very purpose of facilitating such analysis.

Theoretical simplicity and comprehensiveness are the main characteristics of the present approach, for it is based on only three pairs of concepts: inputs and outputs, ends and means, "ego" and "alter" foreign policy. These three pairs of concepts are comprehensive and form an integrated system; no other category may be added arbitrarily to this system without impairing its logical structure. But the system of determinants of foreign policy is, of course, susceptible to further refinement through the addition of other distinctions.

The theoretical simplicity of the scheme does not mean that it is necessarily simple in practice; in no way does it fail to do justice to the complexity of international life. Everything that is summarized under the heading of "policies of other states" alone may represent the policies of dozens of states and the working of the international system. The ele-

[12] The two groups of determinants do not appear to be entirely exclusive. In particular, some of the external interests and power-inputs of one state may be, at the same time, the objectives and power-outputs of other states. (Thus military aid is power-output of the donor, and power-input of the recipient.) But, once recognized, this overlapping of concepts need not be confusing. The need to distinguish between the ego-state's foreign policy (as the reference point for analysis) and the policies of other states is not thereby invalidated.

ments of a single state's foreign policy are far from simple either, and the analysis of any one of them requires considerable insight. However, without obscuring the essential complexities of international relations, the scheme of the determinants of foreign policy does direct attention to the fundamental characteristics of all foreign policy.

The definition of determinants of foreign policy summarizes the descriptive portion of the present study, but it can also be restated in terms suitable for the analysis of the dynamics of foreign policy. Dynamic analysis of foreign policy is the analysis of changes in foreign policies. If a foreign policy is determined by its four elements and by the foreign policies of other states, then a change in one of these elements or in the foreign policies of other states must lead to a change in that foreign policy. Furthermore, since the foreign policies of *other* states are also determined by their four elements, we can say that a foreign policy varies as the result of the changes either in its own four elements or in the elements of the foreign policies of other states. Foreign-policy analysis is the analysis of the causes and effects of changes in the elements of foreign policy.

At this point we repeat emphatically that the dynamic analysis of foreign policy is the analysis of *changes* in foreign policy. Our aim is to determine the ways in which a foreign policy can change the policies of other states and is itself influenced by these policies. Dynamic analysis is concerned *solely* with *changes* in foreign policies; stable foreign policies do not give rise to problems for foreign-policy analysis. A problem arises when one of the elements of a foreign policy undergoes a change.

Implicit in this exclusive concern with the analysis of changes is a "law of inertia" providing that a process of action, including interaction among a plurality of actors, will tend to proceed unless impeded or deflected—unless a disturbance is introduced into the system. In his analysis of the social system,

Talcott Parsons allows for *"no* class of mechanisms for *maintaining* a stable motivational process in operation."* He assumes that "the *continuance* of a stabilized motivational process in a stabilized relationship to the relevant objects is to be treated as *not problematical."* "This assumption . . . ," he claims, "may be compared to the first Newtonian law of motion, the law of inertia, which states that the *problems* for mechanics concern *not* what makes bodies move, but what makes them *change* their motion, in direction or velocity. We shall assume the motivational counterpart of the law of inertia in the present discussion, that it is change of intensity or 'direction'. . . of action which poses the problems for the dynamics of action theory."[13] The present part of this study deals with the disturbances introduced into the system of foreign policies (that is, changes in the elements of foreign policy) and the effects of these disturbances.

The natural complement of the law of inertia is the proposition that every change in foreign policy must be traceable to a disturbance, to additional inputs or to reduced outputs— that is, to changes in the actions that make up foreign policies.[14] From the point of view of any one state, such changes can be of two kinds: *induced,* or *self-generated.* An induced change in one of the elements of a foreign policy is a change that is either the effect of variations in other elements of that foreign policy or the result of the actions of another state. Thus power-input may be increased through external aid or it may suffer curtailment through the defeat of an ally. These

[13] Talcott Parsons, *The Social System* (Glencoe, Ill.: The Free Press, 1951), p. 204. (Parsons' italics.)

[14] As Talcott Parsons, Robert F. Bales, and Edward A. Shils put it: "We assume a *principle of acceleration* which asserts that changes of rate of process must be accounted for by 'forces' operating on (or in) the unit(s) in question. An increase of rate implies an 'input' of energy from a source outside the unit in question, and a decrease of rate, a loss of energy, an 'output' of some sort from the unit." They point out that this principle resembles closely the third law of classical mechanics, the law of acceleration. *Working Papers in the Theory of Action* (Glencoe, Ill.: The Free Press, 1953), p. 165.

are examples of externally induced change in an element of foreign policy. Such changes can also be internally induced: A change in interests expressed to the policy-makers may lead to a change in the objectives of foreign policy; or, a reduction in power-input (a budget cut) may lead to a change in power-output (curtailment of foreign-policy operations). On the other hand, the change in the element of foreign policy may be self-generated—that is, due to spontaneous changes within that element, to changes that are unrelated to variations in the policies of other states, or in other elements of the same policy. Thus, elections may bring to power a new government and change the country's interests; an industrial depression may reduce a country's power-input. The two types of change, the induced and the self-generated changes, may be interwoven; social unrest based on local conditions may be fostered and stimulated from abroad. But, for analytical purposes, changes in an element of foreign policy must be accounted for either by forces operating *on* that element (induced changes), or by forces operating *within* that element (self-generated changes).

Such are the *causes* of changes in the elements of a foreign policy. The question arises: What are the *effects* of changes in an element of foreign policy? The answer is implied in the distinction, just drawn, between internally and externally induced changes in the elements of foreign policy. An *internally* induced change is one that is caused by a variation in another element of the same foreign policy (for instance, a change in objectives caused by changes in interests of the same policy). It follows that one effect of a change in an element of a foreign policy is to induce changes in other elements of the same foreign policy. An *externally* induced change in an element of foreign policy is one caused by a variation in the foreign policy of another state (such as an increase in power-input as the result of external military assistance). It follows that another effect of changes in an element of foreign policy is to induce changes in the foreign policies of other states (and their elements). Hence we say that a change in an element of foreign policy has both internal and external effects.

The preceding argument is based on the assumption that the determinants of foreign policy are interdependent. A change in one element of foreign policy affects all other elements of foreign policies, as indeed it must.[15] If a foreign policy is to undergo a change, it is not sufficient that one of its elements should be altered; the other elements have to change, too. A change in foreign policy may be said to have taken place only after all the elements of foreign policy have been adjusted to the change in one element. Lack of adjustment spells danger to the internal efficiency and to the external effectiveness of a policy.

We can now draw a distinction between internal and external interdependence of elements of foreign policy. Internal interdependence is the interdependence of the four elements of the foreign policy of one state. Because of internal interdependence, a change in an element of a foreign policy is followed by adjustments in the three other elements of that foreign policy. The processes by which a change in one element induces variations in the three other elements of the same foreign policy may be called *internal adjustment*. External interdependence is the interdependence of all foreign policies. Because of external interdependence, changes in one foreign policy affect other foreign policies. The processes by which a change in an element of foreign policy induces modifications in the foreign policy of other states may be called *external adjustment*. Processes of internal adjustment serve to

[15] In the formulation of Parsons, Bales, and Shils: "We conceive of process as occurring in a system which is treated as a point of reference. The system operates through the interaction of its member units. Every change of state of one unit . . . will affect all the other units in the system and in turn the effects of these on the other units will 'feed back' to the original unit. We conceive here of an unbroken 'circular' process of interdependence which is analyzed in terms of the concept of equilibrium." *Ibid.*, p. 167.

keep a policy internally stable and balanced. Processes of external adjustment are the *raison d'être* of foreign policy, for they are the processes by which a community's "foreign-policy problem" is dealt with. A foreign policy may be said to be in equilibrium if all four of its elements are adjusted to each other (internally), and to the foreign policies of other states (externally). The two problems of internal and external adjustment are separable only for analytical purposes, for, as we know, every foreign-policy measure has both internal and external effects. Efforts to influence the policies of other states necessitate the readjustment of the internal equilibrium and, vice versa, efforts arising out of internal adjustment affect the external equilibirium of foreign policy. Internal and external adjustment are the two major problems of the dynamic analysis of foreign policy.

Changes in an element of foreign policy not only set in motion adaptive processes in other elements of foreign policy, but also give rise to reactions aimed at reversing the initial change.[16] Processes that tend to bring about the adaptation of other elements of foreign policies to changes in one element are defined as *positive adjustment*. In contrast, there are processes that tend to neutralize and to reverse changes in elements of foreign policy and to restore the previous equilibrium; these may be defined as *negative adjustment*.

There are certain changes, such as increases in power-input or favorable developments in the policies of other states, to which foreign policy commonly adapts itself without difficulty. There are other changes, such as loss of power-input or the expression of a hostile demand, an ultimatum, by another

[16] Discussing equilibrium problems in social systems, Parsons, Bales, and Shils say: "Once a disturbance has been introduced into an equilibrated system there will tend to be a reaction to this disturbance which tends to restore the system to equilibrium. . . . We may suggest hypothetically that not only is the reaction opposite in direction to the disturbance, but that it is in some sense quantitatively equal in motivational force." This generalization they consider directly parallel to the law of action and reaction in mechanics. *Ibid.*, p. 100.

state, that it may be impossible to prevent and that may have to be suffered. Positive adjustment of elements of foreign policy is the response to such changes.

There are others to which opposition is usual. Reductions in power-input or interference with foreign-policy operations, excessive demands, and unattainable or incompatible objectives usually encounter resistance. Attempts may be made to restore the *status quo ante* by such methods as seeking to increase power-input in other ways, devoting more power-output to endangered operations, or protesting and campaigning against the adoption of undesirable objectives. Part or all of the effects of the initial change in an element of foreign policy may thus be averted through negative adjustment.

Most often, the reaction to a change in an element of foreign policy is mixed, first, because the ways in which interests are affected by it may vary—some sections of the community working for a positive, and others for a negative, adjustment; second, because the power available may not be sufficient to re-establish the desired *status quo ante* (i.e., to effect a completely negative adjustment). After all negative adjustment measures have been taken, the original situation may be partly restored, but some positive adjustment to the change is often required, too. Thus a country experiencing a reduction in power-input due to blockade may have to adjust some of its activities to the scarcities enforced upon it, but it may also partly counteract its effects by tapping new resources of skills and materials. Whether the final adjustment position is positive or negative is determined by the aims and power situation of the concrete case.

Changes Within Policy Elements

The definition of a change in foreign policy basic to dynamic analysis involves the notion of changes (induced or self-generated) in (or within) policy elements.

Policy elements have been conceived of as aspects of the ongoing series of input-output activities that make up foreign policy. But as inputs and outputs, or, in other words, as aspects of actions, policy elements can be viewed as being composed of unit components. Parts II and III have been accounts of the components of which inputs and outputs, interests, objectives, and power consist.

Changes in an element of policy occur whenever a component is added to or subtracted from it. Thus, power-input rises when policy-makers receive additional power-contributions (through the call-up of national servicemen, or through foreign aid); their power-input declines when these are withdrawn. The output of objectives changes when policy-makers adopt a new objective (when they decide to seek to convene an international conference) or when they abandon an objective (for instance, by making a concession). Changes in policy elements can be traced back to changes in components of the inputs and outputs that together make up foreign policy.

The matter of changes in policy elements would be a simple one were it not for the fact that changes within policy elements—that is, the addition or subtraction of a component—affect the remaining components of a policy element. Policy elements are aspects of interdependent systems of activities; these activities are coordinated. Thus the foreign-policy operations of the armed forces must be coordinated with those of the diplomatic services; if they are not, their efforts may overlap or cancel each other out. To take an unlikely case, policy-makers whose armies are engaged in fighting a country cannot instruct their diplomatic service to lend political or other support to that state. Just as there is a need for adjustment of the four policy elements, so the various components of every policy element must also be coordinated. Thus policy-makers cannot act in accordance with the interests of both of two groups or states that are deadly enemies of each other;

these are likely to make contradictory claims on their behavior. It follows that the addition or subtraction of a component in a policy element must be followed by certain adjustments in other components of that element. We shall now inquire into the nature of these adjustments, beginning with the changes effected in the input of interests as the result of the adoption or the abandonment of any one interest.

A change in interests takes place within a framework of basic agreement and compatibility of a community's interests. The acceptance of a new interest has two consequences for other interests: It changes them in a similar direction, and it displaces those that are incompatible. On the other hand, the new interest must accommodate itself to the established interests or it may itself fail to gain acceptance because of its incompatibility with them.

How does the acceptance of a new interest bring about changes in the effective demands of other sections of the community? If an interest is important and persistent enough, it assumes the character of a principle and in time commands widespread and unquestioned support. Sections of the community that rely on the support of groups advancing a new interest will give their backing to it and make it their own. An interest may contain features that make it acceptable to other groups. Lastly, vertical pressures ensure a further stabilization of a new interest. On the other hand, there are processes that prevent interests incompatible with the new interest from remaining acceptable to policy-makers. Being incompatible with the new ruling principles, losing the support of previously allied groups, being given up by foreign-policy organizations or interest groups as the result of "vertical" pressure, interests that are in conflict with the new developments tend gradually to be eliminated. We can illustrate by reference to the "policy of liberation" of the United States in 1952–53. Briefly, it was the wish of certain groups of Americans, accepted for a time by policy-makers, to step up United States activities aimed at the liberation of Eastern Europe from Soviet domination. A persuasion and propaganda campaign was set in motion; a new principle of American foreign policy—"liberation of the enslaved nations"—emerged, and the Republican Party accepted it in its platform. After the 1952 Presidential election, the interest gained a stronger foothold among policy-makers and in foreign-policy organizations. At the same time, the policy of containment began to lose vigor and acceptance; some groups began to withdraw their support from it, and members of foreign-policy organizations too prominently associated with it were virtually dismissed or moved to new positions, while others changed their minds.

In the process of readjustment of interests, it is not only the remaining interests that adjust themselves to the emergence of a new interest. The established interests exert a very definite influence on a new interest, and we must also conceive of the limiting case in which a newly adopted interest is abandoned because of its incompatibility with the established interests. A new interest must adapt itself to the generally accepted principles of foreign policy and to the prevailing alignments of interests. And, returning to the example of "liberation," in the latter part of 1953 it could be observed how the original demands of the "liberators" had begun to adapt themselves to other American interests, including the demands of the United States' allies. *Mutatis mutandis*, the same considerations apply to the abandonment of an interest.

Components of power-input are interdependent, because power-input is not just the sum total of useful services, but a system of activities required for the pursuit of foreign policy. Depending on the foreign-policy operations to be pursued, certain proportions must be established between inputs. Governments require complementary services from a variety of sources. Policy-makers cannot expect to pursue a successful policy by relying solely on the services of their armed forces. Successful conduct of foreign-policy operations requires the coordinated effort of all foreign-policy organizations, the backing of the internal community, the aid and support of external allies, and, finally, the application of power-resources and even the assumption of power-liabilities. Each one of these components of power-input is a necessary ingredient of effective operations. An excess of one of these ingredients, exclusive reliance on another, deficiency in several components of power-input—none of these would be conducive to effective policy. If, therefore, an increase occurs in one component of power-input, there is a strong case for supporting increases in other components in order to make the best of the original increment. For instance, if a country acquires the use of bases in an allied state, it must create an organization for running these bases and mobilize other types of power-input (matériel supplies, transport services, etc.) to obtain the maximum benefit from them. To take another example, it is now recognized that foreign aid (in the form of supplies of equipment and matériel) alone cannot sustain or restore the power of a country if that country is deficient in other components of power-input, such as efficient foreign-policy organizations, the support of the internal community, etc. Complementarism of power-inputs—that is, the necessity for a number of complementary contributions to power-input—is one aspect of the interdependence of power-inputs; interchangeability of power-inputs is another. Interchangeability means that no one single power-input is absolutely indispensable, that shortages in one component of power-input, such as foreign bases, may be compensated for by greater reliance on others—for instance, on alliances. The services derived from newly created power-resources, such as fortifications, an atomic weapons stockpile, or an alliance, may enable a country to dispense with part of its ground forces. In certain cases, an additional power-contribution may thus enable policy-makers to dispense with other power-contributions. Power-inputs are thus linked both by complementarism and by interchangeability.

Changes occur in the output of objectives whenever policy-makers adopt new objectives or abandon established ones. Objectives are one aspect of actions of policy-makers, and the behavior that policy-makers adopt in one set of situations must influence their behavior in other situations. Above all, objectives must be compatible with one another. Policy-makers cannot simultaneously aid and fight another state. They cannot make territorial claims against a state or instigate subversion in it and at the same time expect to receive support from it. At times, objectives may in fact be incompatible, especially when some operations are shrouded in secrecy or when coordination is hampered by their sheer size and complexity. Objectives must not only be mutually consistent and compatible, but they must also positively support one another. Objectives of a smaller scope may be instrumental in the realization of a larger objective. No objective can be pursued in isolation; objectives must so fit together as to form a mutually supporting universe of action.

The adoption of an objective thus tends to eliminate incompatible objectives and to generate new supporting ones. On the other hand, the change may be counteracted by negative processes: The newly adopted objective may be partly or totally incompatible with the traditional objectives of a foreign policy and may be so ill-suited to supporting these objectives, or to being supported by them, that it has to be adjusted or even totally abandoned.

The concept of change in a component of power-output is defined as an increase or decrease in the amount of power-output allocated to, and incurred in, the pursuit of a foreign-policy operation. A change in power-output is a change in the size and distribution of power-output, or—what amounts to the same thing—a change in the cost of policy operations.

The components of power-output are interdependent because of the scarcity of power. Since there is not enough power to implement all desirable objectives, power-output must be carefully apportioned between them. An increase in the rate of power-output incurred in the course of a foreign-policy operation, over and above the planned level (for instance, the steadily rising cost of the Indo-Chinese War to the French after 1949), starve other operations of their due share of power-output (for instance, French commitments in Germany or in North Africa). But a reduction in power-output committed to an operation (a cut in foreign aid or withdrawal of troops from Trieste) makes it possible to assign additional power-output to other tasks (for instance, to the upkeep of the armed forces or to the protection of the Suez Canal Zone). The extent to which an increase or a reduction in the power-output assigned to a policy affects the power-outputs of other policies depends on the interchangeability of the outputs in question. If they are not interchangeable, the reduction of power-output in one policy will not enlarge the amount of resources available for the pursuit of other policies.

Such are, in brief outline, some of the problems of the coordination of the components of policy elements. These problems arise because of the interdependence of the components of one policy element. We shall now turn to an analysis of the relations among the four policy elements themselves.

Internal Adjustment

The present section singles out for special attention and for systematic analysis the problem of internal equilibrium of foreign policy. The existence of the problem has previously been recognized. A number of sophisticated observers and critics of foreign policies have been known to claim that objectives should be determined in the light of the power available for their pursuit, that interests should be related to the resources to be committed to them, and that objectives should be strictly limited by the national interest.

The most eloquent statement of these problems has been

made by Walter Lippmann in his book *U.S. Foreign Policy*. The theoretical focus of this work is

> the compelling and, once seen, the self-evident common principle of all genuine foreign policy . . . the principle that in foreign relations, as in all other relations, a policy has been formed only when commitments and power have been brought into balance. . . . Without the controlling principle that the nation must maintain its objectives and its power in equilibrium, its purposes within its means and its means equal to its purposes, its commitments related to its resources and its resources adequate to its commitments, it is impossible to think at all about foreign affairs. . . . A foreign policy consists in bringing into balance, with a comfortable surplus of power in reserve, the nation's commitments and the nation's power. The constant preoccupation of the true statesman is to achieve and maintain this balance. . . . The statesman of a strong country may balance its commitments at a high level or at a low. But whether he is conducting the affairs of Germany . . . or the affairs of Switzerland . . . he must still bring his ends and means into balance. If he does not, he will follow a course that leads to disaster.[17]

In *U.S. Foreign Policy*, Lippmann contended that prior to 1941, the United States had failed to maintain its *power* at the level required by its aims. He did not investigate the alternative possibility that, perhaps, the United States' *aims* might have been too ambitious in view of the level of available power and should, therefore, have been reduced. Since his was a book of immediate practical import, he did not thoroughly explore the working of principles whose existence he had discussed so persuasively.

Proceeding along similar lines, our analysis of internal adjustment starts from the assumption of the interdependence of the four elements of a foreign policy. The interdependence of these elements has been a thread running throughout this

---

[17] *U.S. Foreign Policy: Shield of the Republic* (Boston: Little, Brown and Company, 1943), pp. 6, 7, 9, and 10.

study. In the section "On Power," we pointed out the ways in which power-input is related to power-output. In the section "On Aims," we observed the links between interests and objectives. The starting point of the present inquiry is thus the assertion that a change in one of the elements involved in a foreign policy sets in motion processes that lead to changes in the remaining elements of that foreign policy. For instance, let us assume that policy-makers have decided to adopt and pursue a new objective. Let us say that American policy-makers have decided to act to prevent the Vietminh from absorbing all of Indochina. This decision affects the three remaining elements of their policy in one way or another, positively or negatively. The change in objectives affects their power-input, because some output has to be transferred to operations connected with the new objective; troop movements and fleet dispositions have to be altered, increased aid and support for Vietnam may be called for, and the supporting action of allies will be invoked. Interests, too, are affected, for the new objective may be in accord with the wishes of some members of the community but contrary to the desires of others. Opposition and isolationist groups may oppose new commitments, and allies may prove hesitant. The new operations will require additional power-input. Changes in interests will also cause secondary changes: They will yield additional power-input from the supporters of the new objective, including the power at the disposal of the existing enemies of Vietminh, but power-input derived from friends of the Vietminh will be reduced. In this way, none of the three elements of a foreign policy remains unaffected by a change in objectives. These elements may be affected positively (they become adjusted to initial change) or negatively (no change occurs), but all three of them are affected by the initial change, and the success of that change depends on the degree to which positive adjustments in the three remaining elements can be effected.

Since foreign policy is determined by four elements (power-input, interests, power-output, objectives), there is a case for analyzing all the logically possible relations among these four elements, for an equilibrium is not established unless the three other elements are adjusted to the initial change in one element of a foreign policy. In a system of four elements, only six modes of relationship among them are possible: interests–power-input; interests–objectives; interests–power-output; power-input–power-output; power-input–objectives; objectives–power-output. We will now explore each one of these relations in turn.

The value of the ensuing analysis lies in the systematic way in which the problem is stated. Consistent with the definition of foreign policy as a system of actions, consistent with the description of dynamic analysis as the analysis of changes in these actions, we put, and seek to answer, the question: What actions have to be performed if a change in one element of a foreign policy is not to upset the internal equilibrium of that foreign policy? The answer is: The three other elements of that foreign policy must be adjusted to that change, or else the policy must be reversed. We are not primarily interested in what an equilibrium is, but in how it is established, how the effects of a change in an element of foreign policy can be forecast, and how the required adjustments are in fact effected.

The first of these relationships links *interests and power-input*. What effect does a change in interests have on the power-input of a foreign policy, and, vice versa, what effect does a change in power-input have on interests?

The interdependence of aims and power is one of the basic tenets of this study. In particular, it can be contended that power, in the sense of services rendered to policy-makers, is a function of the aims of those who exercise power and of the degree to which the aims are satisfied. All expressions of interest carry an implicit, if not explicit, assurance of support and/or threat of withdrawal of present or promised power-input. But interests are linked to power-input in another—and just as compelling—manner, for the importance attached to an interest is a function of the power-contribution associated with it, if only for the good reason that the implementation of an interest must in the first place be assured by additional supplies of power-input. Unsupported by power-input, interests remain idle dreams; unrelated to interests, power-input is wasted.

And that is why a change in interests, such as the adoption of a new demand, may be expected to lead to corresponding changes in power-input—that is, to an increase in contributions from those who uphold that interest. By the same token, the abandonment of an interest by policy-makers reduces the power-input supplied to them by those who uphold it. The process operates in reverse, too: An increase in power-input from a certain source, a rise in the value and importance of a power-contribution, strengthens the claims that such contributors choose to make on policy-makers. Furthermore, an increase in the availability of power creates conditions in which new interests can assert themselves because it makes additional interests susceptible of being realized.

We have just described how interests and power-input may be positively adjusted to each other. But we must also take into account the possibility of negative adjustment. An attempted change in interests may fail to evoke a positive adjustment in power-input and may thus be doomed to ineffectiveness. Or else, a change in power-input may not lead to change in interests; on the contrary, it may set in motion processes that cancel out the original change in power-input, either because the threatened interests are too important to be abandoned, or because the opportunity for new initiative offered by the growth in power-input remains unused. The *status quo ante* in power-input is thus restored.

The formulation of interests and the procurement of power-input are two of the functions of policy-makers, and must be coordinated by them. The importance of this coordination can be seen if one considers the possibility of a failure of the adjustment process. Groups or states that clamor for the adoption of an interest (for France, at one time, control over the Red River Delta in Indochina), without at the same time being willing to furnish additional power-input (e.g., through conscription, to make possible the use of ground troops), cannot be said to be striving for a stable or successful policy. Prudent statesmen keep their aims and aspirations safely within the power that their country possesses or is ready and willing to master. The abandonment of an interest without a change in power-input creates bitterness among the supporters of that interest. An increase in power-input without an adjustment of interests wastes power. Failure to adjust interests to a reduction in power-input fosters illusions of grandeur.

We shall next consider the relations between *interests and objectives*. What changes in objectives are associated with changes in interests, and vice versa?

The "interest-objective" relation is simple, because it describes the link between the claims made on policy-makers in respect of foreign policy and those claims that the policy-makers themselves make on other states. The link between the two policy elements may best be characterized as one of "fulfillment": Objectives represent the practical fulfillment of the interests of the community, the translation of vague urges or firmly held desires into concrete foreign-policy operations. While interests may be imprecise, incoherent, or even unformulated, objectives should be well defined, coordinated, and converted into orders, requests, and recommendations. The transition from interests to objectives is one from desire to fulfillment. Interests will have been fulfilled, or satisfied, in so far as policy-makers succeed in inducing other states to behave in a manner considered desirable by the community. Desirable behavior has been expressed to policy-makers in the form of interests and can be obtained only by being translated into objectives of foreign policy. Interests supply the contents of objectives; objectives give form and discipline to interests. Both are expressed in terms of the desirable behavior of other states, but as a rule interests are not expressed on the same level of generality as objectives. Interests may be couched in wide and general terms, such as "defense of the territorial integrity of the United States," and may give rise to many and varied objectives, such as those implicit in orders to send an army to this or that place, against this or that enemy. Co-ordination of interests and objectives remedies the vagueness and indefiniteness of interests and relates a multitude of foreign-policy operations, and their objectives, to the things wanted and demanded by the community.

Changes in interests bring parallel changes in objectives: The adoption of an interest leads to the definition of new objectives or to the redefinition of existing ones. The abandonment of an interest leads to the abandonment of objectives pursued in implementation of such an interest. In the same way, changes in objectives bring changes in interests. By discontinuing the pursuit of an objective, policy-makers give notice that they have abandoned interests that they previously sought to uphold. The adoption of a new objective gives to policy-makers the support of those who favor such a course of action and, consequently, changes their interests.

Negative adjustments must be mentioned, too. Policy-makers may be unwilling or unable to translate some of the wishes and desires of their community into action and may induce their community to withdraw them. Or else, if policy-makers adopt new objectives without being able to convince their community of the correctness or desirability of such action, they may merely succeed in arousing a storm of opposition and be forced to abandon their plans.

The lines of communication by means of which interests are transformed into objectives are exceedingly complex, for they include political parties and pressure groups, parliaments and other representative institutions, liaison and coordinating committees, the government and its officials, and, finally, the foreign-policy organizations. Nevertheless, policy-makers are the chief actors in this process: They bear the main responsibility for the adjustment of interests and objectives, and it is they who are blamed when inability or unwillingness to adjust results in serious instabilities in foreign policy. A publicly announced change in interests that is not reflected in objectives leaves the policy-makers open to charges of duplicity and betrayal of promises, undermines the confidence of the community, and runs the risk of all the sanctions that a displeased, disappointed, or misled community may choose to apply. When interests are abandoned without this fact being reflected in changes in objectives—for instance, when a newly elected government continues to pursue the "discredited" policy of its predecessors—the affected groups are never slow in voicing their objections and criticisms. A government that changes its objectives without any reference to the wishes and desires of its community cannot rely on wide support in any of its activities. The interest-objective relation is thus at the crux of relations between policy-makers and their community. In a true sense, it is the lifeline of foreign policy, for it lends meaning and purpose to the diffuse and complex activities of large-scale organizations. A disturbance in this lifeline produces little immediate damage, but it is deadly over the long run.

We now turn to the analysis of relations between *interests and power-output*. What are the changes produced in power-output by changes in interests?

The connection between interests and power-output may be described as that linking the desire, on the one hand, and the exact cost—the detailed course—of its implementation, on the other. Interests are tied to power-output by, above all, feasibility. Besides being frequently vague in its claims, the community may also be misinformed about the practicability of its foreign-policy proposals, and that is why interests have to

be related to the concrete prospects of their realization—
prospects that depend on the amount of power-output to be
expended in their pursuit. The confrontation of interests with
power-output requirements brings the community face to face
with the realities of international life. Such confrontation, a
frequent task of policy-makers, heavily taxes the ability and
the courage of all governments.

The adoption of an interest has as its consequence an increase in power-output. The abandonment of an interest, on
the other hand, necessarily leads to a reduction in power-output. Elementary though they may be, these generalizations
belong to the framework of general theory.

Changes in power-output lead to parallel changes in interests.
A reduction in power-output (effected, for instance, through a
cut in budget expenditures) reduces the number of interests
that can be satisfied by foreign-policy operations. Thus a cut
in a previously agreed foreign-aid program affects adversely the
interests of a friendly state. An increase in power-output affects
interests in the opposite way: It makes possible, and lends
vigor to, the pursuit of broader interests.

Changes in interests need not always be followed by adjustments in power-output. If all available power-output is committed to existing policies, no power-output may be available
for policies in furtherance of new interests. Again, the community may not agree to changes in power-output and to the
consequent adjustment of interests and may demand the res-
toration of the original level of power-output. These are cases
of negative adjustment, where a change in one element involved in foreign policy is prevented by processes emanating
from another such element.

An excess of power-output over interests leads to a purpose-
less waste of resources. An excess of interests over power-output (that is, failure to increase power-output following the
adoption of an additional interest, or inability to abandon an
interest following reductions in power-output) is not conducive

to stability either; it arouses criticisms and creates dissatisfaction.

Relations between *power-input and power-output* are centered around the transformation of the one into the other.

The size of a government's power-input is the measure of resources available to it for the pursuit of foreign policy. For its power-output, the government can draw solely on its power-input. The extent of that input provides the limits within which power-output must be accommodated. On the other hand, the shape that output takes influences in its turn the requirements for input components: Prolonged military operations demand a different type of power from multilateral negotiations.

An increase in power-input brings a corresponding increase in power-output. This means that whenever policy-makers have additional resources put at their disposal, they are able to enlarge the scale of their operations. A reduction in power-input is followed by a decrease in power-output and by a contraction of foreign-policy operations. An increase in power-output that is occasioned, for example, by a sudden diplomatic crisis, and that may initially be met out of accumulated reserves, in the end usually brings in its wake a parallel rise in power-input. A fall in power-output resulting, for example, from a relaxation of international tension will be followed by a fall in power-input, if only because the community tends to keep an eye open for opportunities to reduce the burdens of foreign policy.

Postive adjustment is not always the rule. An increase in power-input need not lead to a rise in power-output, for there may be no opportunities for new operations. Power-input will then tend to fall again. Exigencies of policy may not permit a decrease in power-input to cause a reduction in power-output. Finally, power-input may be unresponsive to change in power-output. Planned or attempted increases in output may be quite beyond the bounds of national capabilities.

A state can be said to be living beyond its means when its output is allowed to exceed its input. Such a condition can never persist for long. Another case of failure of coordination of the two elements would be an excess of power-input over power-output, but this might be conducive to the creation of reserves.

Among the internal adjustment problems, the interaction of *power-input and objectives* has received the most attention in the literature, a number of authors stressing the necessity for all nations to limit their objectives in view of the scarcity of available power. Sweeping objectives should never be proclaimed unless the power required to implement them is mobilized at the same time. But the practical problems of relations between objectives and power-input are not exhausted by such considerations. In many cases, it is wrong to consider available power as an immutable datum to which objectives must be automatically adjusted. Policy-makers know that by pursuing objectives enjoying widespread support they can enlarge their power-input.

An increase in power-input leads to the adoption of new objectives. These are not so much "new" as they are objectives that had been kept on the waiting list and now are moved to a priority classification. A decrease in power-input causes the abandonment of some objectives and reduced emphasis on others. If the policy-makers wish to adopt new objectives, they must first make sure that they will obtain the required additional power-input from those interested in the objectives. Whenever they decide to abandon an objective, their requirements for power-input will decline and they will receive less of it. All these processes may also take a negative turn. Thus a decrease in power-input, such as a reduction in the taxes paid by the population, may lead to such a demonstrable decline in the effectiveness of policy that objectives are not affected for long, and power-input is restored to its previous level. A decision to pursue new objectives may be frustrated by an inability to obtain larger power-contributions.

An adjustment, be it positive or negative, is preferable to no adjustment at all. When objectives outrun resources, failure ensues. Nor can a policy be described as efficient (as American policy was after World War I) whose available power is in excess of objectives.

The last of the internal adjustment problems arises as the result of the relations between *objectives and power-outputs*. This concerns, above all, the policy executive who must fashion his objectives by reference to their probable cost in terms of power-output, and who must organize his output for the successful pursuit of a set of objectives. Conceived in budgetary and financial terms, this process requires relating, for instance, various levels of military expenditures to definable capabilities and objectives. Conceived in human terms, it calls for close contacts chiefly between the policy-maker's foreign-policy organizations and their equivalents in friendly states. Essentially, it is the coordination of two policy-making functions: the definition of objectives and the distribution of power-output.

Adoption of new objectives leads to increased power-output; abandonment of objectives, to reduced power-output. Increased power-output is equivalent to the pursuit of new objectives, while the attainment of certain objectives is rendered impossible by a reduction in power-output. Negative adjustments of this kind are equally plain. New objectives can have little effect unless power-output is augmented, nor will the promised or proclaimed abandonment of objectives be credible or become effective unless output is reduced or redistributed. Changes in power-output may be frustrated or remedied by unwillingness or inability to adapt objectives to such changes.

Failure to coordinate objectives with power-output is peculiarly damaging to the effectiveness of foreign-policy operations. An excess of objectives over power-output dissipates resources, strains foreign-policy organizations, upsets priorities, and deprives important policies of the resources due to them. Policy-makers who are unable to adjust power-output downward as the result of abandonment of an objective are wasting power for the efficient use of which they are responsible. Failure to adjust objectives and power-output to one another is tantamount to inability to conduct foreign policy efficiently.

We have reached the end of the review of the internal adjustment problems. We have studied the adjustments that changes in one policy element force upon other elements of the same policy. Each one of the six relations among the four policy elements has some special significance, and each one of them has its own specific problems to contend with.

This review presents no more than an outline of what can be said on this subject; it does, however, suffice to show that a change in one element involved in foreign policy induces further changes in the three remaining policy elements. A change in one policy element, such as the abandonment of an objective, simultaneously influences the three other elements— interests, power-input, and power-output—because it is followed by the abandonment of interests, by a fall in power-input, and by reductions in power-output. A change in one policy element may also be countered by negative adjustment processes, and thus, in one way or another, all the elements involved in a foreign policy adapt themselves to changes in one policy element, producing, by their concerted action, a change in foreign policy.

The definition of the determinants of foreign policy introduced at the beginning of this section thus assumes new meaning. The mechanisms of determination and the processes that enable us to say that interests, objectives, power-input, and power-output are among the determinants of foreign policy are now clearer.

Mention has also been made of the instabilities caused by a

malfunctioning of the adjustment process. Generalizing, one can say that it is a condition of the internal stability of a foreign policy that a change in one of its policy elements should be followed by positive or negative internal adjustment processes. A foreign policy has attained internal stability when all of its four elements are in equilibrium. Such being the condition of internal stability, the study of internal adjustment processes leads to what might be called "the laws of internal adjustment." These laws would spell out in greater detail, along the lines just indicated, the various ways of obtaining positive or negative internal adjustment.

External Adjustment

Until now, we have been discussing problems of the internal equilibrium of a foreign policy. But, however efficient, coherent, and coordinated a policy may be internally, it can never divorce itself of its prime function: influencing the behavior of other states. At this stage we shall therefore enlarge the scope of this analysis to include the key problem of the theory of foreign policy and, in some respects, of international relations—namely, the problem of external adjustment. How is a desirable change in the foreign policy of another state brought about? How are the undesirable consequences of the policies of other states minimized? The arguments of the preceding sections were merely so many stepping stones, the preliminary foundations for the discussion of these supreme questions of foreign-policy analysis.

External adjustment, or the quest for external equilibrium, is another chapter in the story of man's attempts to control his environment and of his efforts to adapt himself to it. In the case of foreign policy, the environment consists of the foreign policies of other states. Policy-makers seek to influence the behavior of other states, but they are not omnipotent, even if they are the policy-makers of a world power. Their capacity to change the foreign policies of other states is narrowly circumscribed. Dr. Johnson's lines:

> How small of all that human hearts endure
> That part which kings or laws can cause or cure!

should serve as preface to the study of all foreign policy. Indeed, harm can be done by people who want to know right there and then what will be the guaranteed outcome of every governmental action. The great problems of foreign affairs, it has been said, are close to being part of the problem of nature. They yield only to correct treatment applied steadily and consistently over a long period of time. Even then results are achieved in ways that are unexpected, could scarcely have been foreseen, and are not always recognizable when they occur. We may take this as an injunction to approach external adjustment problems in a spirit of humility.

Admitting, however, the limitations of foreign policy and of foreign-policy analysis, students of the subject would be foolish to go to the other extreme and assert that foreign-policy operations can produce no results, that international affairs are all a matter of chance and in any case too complex to understand and to manipulate. One can sympathize with the policy-makers of small states living under the shadow of a big power. Their ability to influence the conduct of other states may, indeed, be close to nil. But their predicament is not universal. Many small powers pursue an effective foreign policy because of their remoteness from the centers of power or by virtue of special contributions that they make to the resources of their bigger brethren. The middle and the great powers have the capacity to produce important results on the world stage, and they cannot escape responsibility for the way they use it. Aware of the limitations of political action, let us seek to improve the effectiveness of foreign policies, rather than abandon hope of altering the course of world events.

The interdependence of foreign policies and their susceptibilities to mutual influence are among the basic assumptions of international relations, just as they are basic to the analysis of problems of external adjustment. Relations between states arise because the actions of one state have significant effects on the behavior of another state, and, furthermore, because such behavior is often amenable to influence. The phenomenon of external adjustment thus needs no separate explanation.

Processes of external adjustment are those by which changes in a foreign policy induce modifications in the foreign policies of other states. The problem of external adjustment is one of creating externally induced changes in the policy elements of other states. Since each one of the "other" states pursues a foreign policy that can be conceived of as combining four elements, we can distinguish four types of external adjustment processes, according to whether they are concerned with inducing changes in the other states' interests, power-input, objectives, or power-output.

Studying external adjustment, we are also concerned with the reactions of the other states to efforts aimed at changing their interests, power-input, objectives, and power-output. We are not interested in the case in which a state is either totally unwilling or totally unable to react to, and to oppose, external attempts to change the elements involved in its policy. Important, and theoretically more significant, is the case in which the state seeks to nullify, or to minimize the effects of, efforts made to change its foreign policy. Such reaction to "offensive" external policies can be described as "defensive." The distinction between *offensive* and *defensive* reaction is equivalent to positive and negative reactions in internal adjustment. (The terms "offensive" and "defensive" seem more appropriate in the context of external adjustment.) It appears legitimate to describe as "offensive" all positive foreign policies aimed at inducing a change in the policy of another state, while negative policies, which seek to maintain the *status quo* and prevent a change in policy, may then be called "defensive." Corresponding to the four offensive methods of external adjustment are therefore four defensive processes—those that seek to prevent another state from inducing changes in the ego-state's interests, power-input, objectives, and power-output.

In the light of the distinction between offensive and defensive external adjustment, the notion of "external equilibrium" may appear in a new perspective. An external equilibrium has been reached when the offensive actions of a state have been met by the defensive reactions of other states and when the offensive actions of other states have been successfully countered by the ego-state's own defensive reactions. The balance of power, in the sense of a description connoting either the existence or non-existence of equilibrium, can thus be seen as a special case of the dynamics of foreign policy and of external equilibrium; it deals with power only and does not reflect the fact that for external stability an equilibrium must be established not only in respect of power, but also between the aims of states.

We shall now discuss the processes by which changes can be externally induced in every one of the four policy elements. The account is limited to the description of methods of inducing a change in a policy element; at this stage we are no longer concerned with showing how a change in one policy element affects the three other elements, for that has been the subject of the preceding sections dealing with internal adjustment. If one state contrives to change, say, the power-input of another state, we may expect this change to be translated into changes in interests, objectives, and power-output, except in the case of successful negative adjustment. Processes of internal adjustment constitute the mechanism whereby developments on the international scene percolate into the body politic of a community, and that is why we shall not, and need not, be concerned with anything more than externally induced changes in one policy element. We can now see why the analysis of internal adjustment processes is an indispensable component of, and a logical necessity for, foreign-policy analysis; without the concept of internal adjustment we would be unable to explan how foreign policy can be changed by altering one of the policy elements.

The first group of external adjustment processes includes methods of *changing the interests of other states* and the defensive measures that may be taken in response to such actions.

The alteration of the interests of another state must be ranked among the more difficult tasks confronting the makers of foreign policy. The bonds of cooperation and community—of which interests are an outcrop—are among the more persistent features of policies. At times, they appear so formidable, and so suffused with sentiment, that some writers present interests as the immutable data of foreign policy, the inalterable realities of international life. But despite those who ignore the wishes and desires of the community in respect to foreign affairs or reduce them to a few self-evident and nearly meaningless generalities—like, for instance, security or the maintenance of peace—the input of interests can, for all practical purposes, he treated as being as alterable as the other elements involved in a foreign policy. As has been remarked: "The permanent interests of greater powers change according to circumstances."[18]

The input of interests is an aspect of the relations between policy-makers and their community and consists of the demands of members of the internal and external community and of temporary collaborators, and the interests of policy-makers. Hence, the input of interests can be changed if (1) members of the internal and external community change demands in respect to foreign policy; (2) members of the

[18] Georg Schwarzenberger, *Power Politics: A Study of International Society* (2d rev. ed.; New York: Frederick A. Praeger, 1951), p. 49.

internal and external community withdraw from the community; (3) policy-makers change their interests; and (4) unfriendly policy-makers are removed from office and are replaced by friendly policy-makers.

1a. Changing the wishes and desires of the internal community. Through a variety of procedures, "the people" and political groups within the internal community of another state may be made to influence the policy of their own government in line with the objectives of the "offensive" state. President Wilson's unsuccessful appeal to the Italian people over the heads of their government during the Paris Peace Conference is a familiar example of the dangers of this procedure. And yet it is the routine duty of propaganda organizations, of information and press officers, of foreign broadcasting services, and, in part, of diplomatic representatives to state the case of their governments, to underline areas of coincidence of interest, and to influence public opinion on foreign-policy issues; hence the attempts of Soviet "peace" propaganda to create public sentiment for reducing military expenditures and banning atomic weapons, in the hope that foreign governments may ultimately be influenced by it. Similar aims may be sought through the establishment of more intimate and private contacts with groups interested in a more limited range of problems or concerned in obtaining special treatment. Temporary support may thus be obtained from a variety of quarters.

1b. Changing the wishes and desires of the external community. The aim is to alter the policy of a government by prevailing upon its allies to remonstrate with it. Thus a third state may be able to influence the Indian Government to make a suggestion to the British Government. Another country may hope to influence the American Government by having the British Government intercede on its behalf. Policy-makers may also try to appeal in support of their causes to "world public opinion"—in particular, to the United Nations.

2a.   Detaching members of the internal community. "Divide and rule" has long been recognized as an important precept of politics. Efforts to turn soldiers and civilians of enemy countries against their rulers have been made by political leaders since time immemorial. By splitting up a community and detaching groups from it, foreign states are able to change the interests of that community. A community is never perfectly homogeneous; tensions always animate it. Some policy-makers may choose to exploit latent conflicts to their own advantage, and religious, racial, ideological, or national minority conflicts are all liable to be used in this way. By such methods as emphasizing conflict through propaganda, organizing opposition groups and resistance movements, supporting collaborationist or exile governments, and fomenting strikes or civil war, policy-makers may succeed in turning the citizens of a country against their government. They may seek to sow confusion and to weaken the cohesion of a community in order to make it more amenable to pressure, or they may try to create conditions favorable to annexation. Methods whereby policy-makers alter the interests of other communities by detaching groups from the internal community are known as subversion.

2b.   Detaching members of the external community. A traditional field for the exercise of diplomatic skill is altering the composition of rival external communities, winning and keeping allies, and destroying the alliances of the opponent. It is never rational to concede the unity of the enemy camp. No alliance lasts forever, and no member of the external community can ever be taken for granted. A policy-maker's constant preoccupation is to neutralize hostile states and make friends among the neutrals. The great day of a policy-maker comes when he is able to contrive a "diplomatic revolution" and bring about a reversal of international alignments; Talleyrand in 1814–15, Bismarck in 1863–70, and Hitler with his Soviet pact in 1939 were able to achieve just that.

3. Changing policy-makers' interests. Governments serve as the intermediaries between their community and the outside world; other states avail themselves of this fact and seek to influence the policy-makers, so that they themselves will then implement a change in the demands of their community. The functions of policy-makers consist not only of registering and implementing the interests of their community, but also of guiding them and assisting in the formulation of interests; policy-makers have a set of their own interests to take into consideration. This gives to policy-makers a certain freedom of action in the forming of foreign policy; it is an avenue that diplomacy uses in order to change the interests of a community. The media for bringing about changes in policy-makers' interests are negotiations between diplomatic representatives or personal contacts between policy-makers of various countries. Privacy of proceedings is a characteristic feature of such contact, and secret undertakings (like those at Yalta in 1945) are their frequent result. The written instruments, such as treaties and conventions, that are the outcome of most diplomatic contacts sometimes codify existing interests, but more often they modify interests if only because the necessities of negotiation draw the parties into compromise. Upon the conclusion of the process, policy-makers face the task of inducing their community to accept curtailment of interests that may result from the meetings. Ratification of treaties is the formal process through which this task is accomplished, for ratification signifies that policy-makers have succeeded in obtaining the agreement of their community to the steps they have taken. The community's approval may also be expressed in more spontaneous forms, such as the popular satisfaction in Britain with the result of the Munich talks in 1938.

4. Changing policy-makers. Interests can be changed not only through inducing existing policy-makers to adapt their conceptions of interests, but also by replacing the policy-

makers. The replacement of existing policy-makers by new men with different interests at heart is a more thorough way of changing interests than attempting to make the old policy-makers revise their position. For various reasons, they cannot do so easily; they may find it difficult to capitulate to external pressure or "foreign interference"; they are expected to be consistent in their actions and they cannot lightly desert causes with which they have become identified. But although the replacement of "difficult" policy-makers simplifies the conduct of relations between the two countries on the official level, it puts a strain on the relations between the new policy-makers and their internal community. Outside interference with the government creates resentment, and the new government may find it difficult to win popular confidence. But despite this limited effectiveness of intervention in the appointment of policy-makers, attempts are made from time to time to overthrow the government of another state, to interfere with the conduct of elections, to obstruct the assumption of office by "unfriendly"individuals, or to attack and abuse individual members of the government in order to bring about their fall. Germany's demand for the dismissal of Delcassé, the French Foreign Minister during the 1905 crisis; the overthrow of the Egyptian government through British military pressure in 1942; and the careful scrutiny, at Yalta and subsequently, of the political record of Polish politicians from whose ranks the Provisional Government of National Unity was to be formed in 1945, are illustrations of the importance attached to having the right men in the seats of power.

The problem of changing interests has been resolved into that of altering the relations between policy-makers and their community. It follows that the task of preventing undesirable changes in interests consists in strengthening and consolidating these relations. Intimacy of contact between policy-makers and their community is the heart of successful defense against external interference with interests. The strength of the bonds that unite the community is a function of the success with which policy-makers, in their objectives, are satisfying the interests of the community. But the strength of these bonds is not only the result of the efficient performance of their functions by policy-makers; it is also a consequence of belief in common principles. As previously observed, one of the characteristics of principles, as compared with other interests, is their stability. Principled interests are less susceptible to change and outside influence than other interests. Hence, the more the relations between policy-makers and their community are based on principles, the smaller the danger of their being affected by outside interference. Negatively, the strength of the community's bonds is inversely proportionate to the degree of friendship, cooperation, and communication with outside groups. In its preventive and remedial aspects, defense against external interference with interests demands the cultivation of internal cohesion, the nursing of common principles, and control over outside contacts.

Policy-makers find it less easy to keep under control the contacts between members of their external community and third states. But here, too, strong forces tend to check any tendency to listen to outside persuasion. Friendship between countries generates emotions and finds expression in principles. Contact with outsiders, and with enemies in particular, provokes charges of betrayal or treachery to the common cause. Most treaties of alliance and friendship provide for consultation on matters of common interest, and diplomatic custom has it that international conferences should be attended by all interested parties. Many a diplomatic convention has been designed for the express purpose of facilitating communication, even between hostile states; but no device of diplomatic etiquette can easily overcome the obstacles to communication that have been created by a background of hostility, suspicion, and prejudice. Important as open diplomatic channels may be, defensive forces are always at work to prevent the contacts from becoming too close.

The same defensive forces operate, though in a much stronger fashion, against attempts to break up communities and to detach some of their members. The strength of feeling aroused by attempts at subversion is enormous and is testimony to the importance attached to the preservation of communities. Since subversive activities are the province of small organized minorities, their exposure and isolation may be enough to render them harmless if the government can count on the support of large sections of the population. There are fewer safeguards against interference with the external community, but every international friendship and alliance is the work of political groups. The honor of states is said to be involved in the observance of the requirements of international friendship and states do not gain prestige by changing camps frequently.

Isolation can be considered as a defense mechanism, intended to reduce contacts with the outside world to a minimum. In an atmosphere of isolationism, all dealings with the outside world are apt to be viewed with suspicion and the foreign-policy organizations are suspected of representing the foreigner. The ability of other states to influence an isolationist state is therefore limited.

Outside interference with policy-makers stimulates as much ill-feeling and resentment as foreign subversion. If they are fulfilling their duties properly, policy-makers are a crucial organ of the body politic, and the community cannot afford or tolerate any interference with them. By maintaining close links with their community, avoiding internal and external crises, and exposing and isolating the counterelites, policy-makers can minimize the occasions on which external influences can play a part in the choice of the government.

The second group of external adjustment problems concerns method of inducing *changes in the power-input of other states*. In the light of concepts on power developed in Part II, the power-input of policy-makers may be altered by external influences upon (a) current input, (b) power-resources, (c) power liabilities, and (d) the services of policy-makers.

The earlier analysis revealed the important role that external contributions play in power-input. By implication, this analysis has detailed the ways in which the policy-makers of one state may *enlarge* the power-input of the policy-makers of another state. At this point we shall do no more than recall that the chief ways in which one state can enhance the power-input of another state are: actions toward third states in support of the foreign policy of that state; direct support to its foreign-policy organizations; support of its external groups; supplies of matériel and equipment; services of its power-resources; creation of the ego-state's external power-resources; and support given on credit. All policies that enhance the power-input of another state are commonly regarded by it as "friendly."

By contrast, most of the actions concerned with *reducing* the power-input of other states are of the kind that diplomats call "unfriendly" and that usually go under the name of "warfare." It is also true that the enhancement of the power-input of one state by another may be considered an unfriendly act by a third state. "Economic warfare" has been defined as "all actions in either peace or war, military or otherwise, designed to increase our own and our allies' economic strength for security, or to decrease the strength of an enemy's, or a potential enemy's, economy."[19] We have already indicated the methods for increasing the strength of other countries, and our field is wider than that of economic warfare because we are concerned not only with the strength of a country's economy, but also with its total power. We are, nonetheless, concerned with warfare, for the use of the armed forces is an

[19] George A. Lincoln, William S. Stone, and Thomas H. Harvey (eds.), *Economics of National Security* (New York: Prentice-Hall, 1950), p. 460.

important ingredient in all actions whose objective is to reduce the power-input of another state and gives these actions their warlike character. States that aim at destroying another state's foreign-policy organizations, disrupting the life of its community, and cutting its links with the outside world, resort to full-scale war and, if successful, follow it up with the occupation of the defeated state. But the primary task of foreign-political action is not to destroy men but to influence their attitudes and their behavior. Military victory cannot be a substitute for wise and patient political action directed toward the minds of men. A state resorting to warlike methods of pursuing its objectives cannot evade the vast problems created by such drastic measures.

Those who wish to reduce power-input externally must prevent the otherwise willing members of the community from contributing to that power-input. Hence, there are two ways in which power-input can be reduced: the transmission (or transport) lines of power-input may be interrupted, or the power-contributors (supporters) themselves may be rendered ineffectual.

The first step that policy-makers will take if they want to influence the power-input of another state is to see whether their own foreign-policy organizations, and their community at large, are in some way contributing to the power-input of that other state. The ego-state may be assisting the alter-state in its policies, or it may be exporting strategic materials to it. Thus in World War II, a large part of the administrative activities of the British Ministry of Economic Warfare was devoted to ensuring that no contraband goods were being sent to enemy countries from British-controlled territories or with the help of British firms. Having ensured that their own policies in no way augment the power-input of the "unfriendly" state, policy-makers may proceed to seek to reduce that state's internal and external current power-input in other ways.

Current power-input consists of the human and nonhuman

services of the foreign-policy organizations and of the internal community. In what way can external action reduce these services? A state may interfere with the transport and communication systems through which these services are rendered and organized for action. Foreign-policy organizations and the community use, in the main, the same transport systems and other facilities of this sort; interference with these systems therefore affects the power-input from both sources. The services of foreign-policy organizations can be reduced by hindering exchanges between various parts of the organizations, and among the organizations, the policy-makers, and the community. The community's services are transmitted to policy-makers by such systems of activities as the transport network for passenger and goods traffic, the communication systems for the exchange of orders and information, the administrative system of the state, and the taxation and general fiscal and monetary system. Each one of these can be interfered with by outside action. Transport and communication networks may be damaged by sabotage or espionage, by actions of resistance groups or of the armed forces proper. An administrative system is not easily dislodged, but the military occupation of the territory renders it ineffectual. By means of full-scale war, not only are the internal transmission lines of power-input interrupted, but the foreign-policy organizations of a state may be destroyed and its internal community broken up.

The interruption of a state's connections abroad—that is, interference with its external power-input—is known as "blockade." Blockade prevents a state from receiving supplies and services from abroad, makes it more difficult for the state to compensate other states for services they render, and involves negotiations with neutrals for the restriction of the services rendered by them to the enemy. Export and import controls, blacklisting, shipping control, seizure of foreign assets—these are some of the devices used to interrupt communications between an enemy state and those who cooperate with it. Where blockade is of no avail, the external allies of the enemy state can be dealt with only by direct military action.

So much for current power-input. Power-input can also be reduced by interference with assets or resources either through changes in control arrangements or outright destruction. A state loses control of its power-resources when portions of its territory, especially those with strategic, industrial, or other significance, are detached from it. A state may lose power-resources by being forced to evacuate some of its overseas bases, concessions, or colonies. An outside power may succeed in occupying strategic positions inside the state or compulsorily acquire possession of some of its industries. Finally, entire factories and industries may be dismantled and shipped away, just as other movable assets (especially human resources, such as technicians and scientists) may be transferred to another state.

Man has devised many methods of destroying power-resources, those accumulated results of his past exertions. Strategic bombing with atomic weapons is a method of destroying resources par excellence. Naval warfare aims at destroying the opponent's naval craft and merchant marine. The wiping out of fortresses and other fortifications, the destruction of military bases, factories, mines, and ports, are all methods of disarming a defeated enemy. Particularly ruthless regimes do not hesitate to strike at and wipe out the human assets of a community—its leaders, its educated classes, or the officers of its army; they may change the populations of doubtful regions and transplant or annihilate entire nationalities.

Policy-makers obtain some of their power-input on the strength of promises. Propaganda activities throwing doubt on the policy-makers' reliability and prospects may succeed in cutting down this particular source of power-input. Finally, since the quality of policy-makers themselves is a country's important asset, their removal results in a reduction in power-input. Hence some powers may be interested in removing a successful national leader from his position.

Such are, in outline, the methods to which a state resorts in order to reduce another state's power-input. Of methods there are many, but even this brief discussion has shown that few of them can be applied without an exertion of force. In one way or another, they all amount to waging war, hot or cold, declared or undeclared. They all presuppose enmity and arouse further enmity in their application. Nor are they easily applicable in isolation; war has its own inner momentum and once one method of reducing power-input has been embarked upon, the hostile climate it generates lends momentum to other similar measures that, if unchecked, lead to war. War consists of the simultaneous application of all these methods. External interference with power-input has one redeeming feature: Its very dangers prevent its frequent use. The threat of the application of such destructive methods may make their application unnecessary, or else they may provoke such strong countermeasures that their success cannot be guaranteed.

What measures can policy-makers take to defend the power-input of their foreign policy from external interference? There is no other effective reply to force but counterforce, but if that counterforce is to be available at the right moment and in the right amount, power must be stocked long in advance of the time of crisis. Defensive preparations cannot easily be undertaken without a great deal of imaginative insight; it is not without reason that generals are accused of "preparing for the last war." Whatever the shortcomings of British defense preparations in World War II, the reason for the British victory in the Battle of Britain in 1940 lay in the fact that the Royal Air Force had prepared to fight the Battle of Britain long before the war began, but the Germans had not.

Far-sighted power-investment is thus the key to all defense against interference with power-input. Detailed defensive measures are required for the protection, above all, of those

areas of national life that are most vulnerable to hostile action. Lines of communication of all kinds are the object of
special concern to all policy-makers, especially of those with
far-flung internal possessions or external allies. The importance
of the Suez Canal as the point through which pass the life-
lines of the Empire has for a long time impressed British
policy-makers. Britain's efforts in antisubmarine defense are
the result of the vulnerability of her sea communications. The
problem of communication with allied states is one to which
all statesmen devote a great deal of thought, and it accounts
for the tendency of allied states to seek contiguous frontiers.

Another defense against interference with power-input consists in developing sources of power-input alternative to those
that might be endangered by hostile activities. The creation
of reserves is one way of doing that; stockpiles of strategic raw
materials may be accumulated, local sources of raw materials
spared from too early exploitation, or human resources trained
in excess of current needs. A state with a flexible social organization is able to meet the destruction of parts of its foreign-policy organizations, or of portions of its power-resources,
by setting up new organizations and changing the uses of its
remaining power-resources. Although no state can become
entirely autarchic, or totally independent of external power-
input, autarchy is a manner of responding to threats to external power-input; it consists in the development of internal
sources of power-input in an effort to reduce dependence on
external supplies.

Every policy-maker pays special attention to the preservation of the community's power-resources. The preservation of
the integrity of national territory is held to be one of the most
important objects of foreign policy. Other national assets,
such as population, industries, or assets abroad, are equally
jealously guarded; control of them never passes to another
state without great commotion, and much national effort is
expended in their defense.

We come now to the third external adjustment problem. Here the qeustion is: How can one state induce *changes in the objectives of another state?*

The objectives of a foreign policy are a function of the policies of other states because they comprise the envisaged desirable behavior of those states and the foreign-policy operations on the part of the ego-state that are necessary to bring it about. Thus, when the actual behavior of other states changes, objectives (and foreign-policy operations) must be readjusted. Hence, the ego-state may change the objectives of the alter-state's foreign policy by altering its own foreign policy, by (a) abandoning unfriendly policies or adopting friendly policies, or (b) abandoning friendly policies or adopting unfriendly ones.

Policy-makers can alter the objectives of other states by abandoning those of their foreign policies that other states find objectionable. If, let us say, the Soviet Union abandoned her claims on some Turkish provinces and stopped activities aimed at the acquisition of these provinces, then Turkey could be expected to adjust her objectives in connection with measures required for their defense. On the other hand, a state may choose to avoid being the object of hostile acts by adjusting its policy in line with the objectives of the hostile state; thus Turkey could choose to accede to Soviet demands in order to avoid a war. Reluctance to embark on hostile activities against an ally (the sacrifice of a lesser objective in order to gain an ally for a greater one) is a characteristic of all alliances. For example, in World War II, Britain and the United States tended to avoid or postpone the discussion of issues that the Soviet Union might find offensive, such as East European frontier questions.

Policy-makers may be able to alter the objectives of other states by entering upon a course of action agreeable to those states through bargaining. Such bargains may be multilateral —for instance, agreements in which all parties pledge themselves to adopt certain rules of action whereby a change of policy on the part of one state is offset by parallel changes in the objectives of other states (such as the Copenhagen Convention on the allocation of radio wave lengths or the Universal Postal Union). Or else they may be bilateral—for instance, the Treaty of London (1915), in which certain Italian territorial claims were granted in return for Italy's promise to enter the war, or the 1953 American-Spanish agreement, under which Spain secured military aid from the United States in return for bases. Bargains need not always be explicit. By pursuing a policy benefiting a certain state, policy-makers are in a position to exercise pressure on that state in support of their other policies. This ability to put on pressure is related to the threat inherent in all beneficial policies—that is, the possibility that the policy may be stopped. The threat of withdrawal of military or diplomatic support, aid, or other "favors" is another lever that states may use in order to obtain changes in objectives.

Finally, policy-makers may be able to induce changes in the objectives of other states by adopting, or threatening to adopt, unfriendly measures. Through diplomatic protests, the strength of feeling aroused by the objectives a state has been pursuing and the probable consequences of its actions can be brought to the notice of another state. Threats of reprisals may also be conveyed through other than diplomatic channels.

The influencing of objectives is, par excellence, the field of diplomacy and is commonly accomplished through some form of negotiation, conference, or meeting of policy-makers. The task of externally inducing changes in objectives by altering the policy of one's own state is facilitated by the fact that the community's interests admit of expression by more than one set of objectives; for every need there is a range of possible remedies. This may be so for two reasons. The satisfaction of an interest may be possible through a number of types of behavior on the part of other states; thus, British interests in a base on the Suez Canal admit expression in more than one type of control to be wielded by the Egyptians. The American interest in European stability may be realized in a number of different alignments of European powers. Secondly, interests can be satisfied through the pursuit of one out of a number of possible foreign-policy operations. Thus, Britain may be able to protect the Suez Canal base through more than one type of operation. Although these alternative actions are not equally advantageous, they do make for a certain flexibility and provide theoretical justification for the diplomats' eternal search for a "formula."

Not much can be said about defensive adjustments to attempts at changing objectives. In so far as the other state is adopting a friendly policy or is abandoning an unfriendly one, the ego-state has no reason for taking defensive measures. If, on the other hand, these policies are unfavorable, the ego-state may either ignore them, give up all cooperation and refuse to change its objectives, or else it may resort to reprisals and adopt equally unfriendly measures in retaliation.

The fourth and last type of external adjustment process concerns ways of *influencing the power-output of another state*.

The national effort exerted in the pursuit of foreign-policy operations is not only a complex function of interests, power-input, and objectives, but is also dependent on the foreign policies of other states. The power-output of one state is *inter alia* a function of the power-output of other states. Power-outputs are a measure of the tasks confronting a foreign policy, tasks not only set by policy-makers, but also imposed upon a state by the exertions of other policy-makers. Hence one state is able to influence the power-output of another by changing the scale and pattern of its own power-output, because by doing so it alters the tasks confronting that state. Power-output of the alter-state can be influenced by (a) changes in the current operations of the ego-state; (b) changes in the power-investment program of the ego-state; (c) changes in the manner of discharge of the liabilities of the ego-state.

In principle, every change in foreign-policy operations affects the tasks confronting the foreign policies of other states. Thus, a British decision to send a cruiser to the Falklands alters the tasks confronting the Argentine Government. Or, the request of a group of states—say, the Arab-Asian group—for a U.N. debate on Tunis and Morocco, and the lobbying activities that go with it, present France with a diplomatic situation that can be met only by drawing on various resources, including the support of France's allies. Every move on the international scene presents states with a new situation that they must counter by a rearrangement of their resources or by the mobilization of new sources of strength.

Changes in current power-output are effected either through a redistribution of power-output as between policies (by increasing pressure on one state while reducing it on others), or through an over-all increase in the power-output of the ego-state. Partial or total mobilization of the armed forces, troop concentrations in frontier districts, demonstrative military exercises, military aid, fleet movements, the manufacture of frontier incidents, actual military operations, spells of intense diplomatic activity, the wooing of potential allies—all these are instances of increases in the power-output of the ego-state that *ipso facto* put a strain on the power-output of other states.

Power-output is also affected by changes in the power-investment programs and the resources position of other states. By devoting greater amounts of power-output to power-investment, a state increases its future ability to influence other states. Such investment must be suitably countered by other states; otherwise they may find themselves at a disadvantage in the future. Investment offers a variety of ways in which one state may influence the power-output of other states. Rearmament is one of these ways: by forming new military formations; training large cadres; constructing war factories, military installations, and air and naval bases; stockpiling war equipment, food, and atomic weapons—by all these means a state imposes strains on the military services of other states. The development of every weapon alters the value of existing weapons and of accepted military tactics. All industrial construction and accumulation alter future power relations. Investment in the transport and communication networks increases the mobility of power. Foreign aid and other forms of support augment the future power of allied states.

In preference to patiently developing their power-resources over a prolonged period, policy-makers may choose to augment their assets by acquiring control over ready-made assets belonging to other states. They may occupy and perhaps annex another state, whereby much of the power-resources situated on that territory will fall into their hands. Portions of territories may be detached from other states and used for bases or as sources of raw materials. Population groups may be moved. Finally, territories may be bought or exchanged or industrial assets acquired in foreign countries. Naturally, in each of these cases, the state is also acquiring liabilities (an unreliable population, the hostility of neighbors, etc.). It goes without saying that other states cannot remain indifferent to the spectacle of a state enlarging its power-resources at the expense of its neighbors.

Finally, a change in the methods by which a state meets its liabilities—for instance, repudiation of obligations or of promises—also inevitably affects the power-output of other states.

In summary, then, a state changes the power-output of another state by confronting it with additional tasks, by increasing its own power-output and increasing thereby the pressure on the power-output of that state. There is no easy defense against this type of "offensive" external adjustment; it is rightly said that it takes only one to start a war. Isolation can hardly be of avail in this field. Defensive adjustment to external influence on power-output consists in easing as much as possible the strain on foreign policy, replying in kind, and demonstrating the ineffectiveness of the challenge. This is achieved by instantaneous reaction to all changes in the international situation, development of input, and the expansion of resources.

We have now dealt, though only in an introductory fashion, with the principal methods whereby a state can influence the foreign policy of another state by inducing a change in one of the elements involved in that policy. And it may be repeated at this point that a state can change the course of the policy of another state by altering either its interests, its power-input, its objectives, or its power-output. It has now also been shown in what way, precisely, the foreign policy of one state may be said to be determined by the foreign policy of another state.

The outline study of the adjustment processes of foreign policy is hereby concluded. The essence of the present chapter can be put as follows: Every foreign-policy action may be conceived of as a change in one of the elements involved in the foreign policies that together compose the international system. Every such action affects all the other parts of the international system; the adjustment processes are the three main dimensions of the impact of the change on other parts of the international system. A change within an element involved in one foreign policy alters other components of that element; a change in one element involved in a foreign policy alters the other three elements involved in that policy; and, finally, changes in the foreign policy of one state affect other foreign policies. Hence, the analysis of adjustment processes provides the theoretical model for what has been called "total field policy," which leads to a revaluation of the whole field when one of the component parts of the field has had its value changed.

The Balance Sheet of Policy

We have traveled almost the whole way and are now near the end of our analysis. One more point deserves some mention: the problem of appraising policy and its effects.

So far, we have been preoccupied with foreign policy viewed *ex ante*, with the planning and formation of foreign policy rather than with its final product. Both interests and objectives refer to the effects of policy, but by their nature they describe intended effects rather than achieved results. There is no reason to suppose that intentions as a rule correspond to the actual effects of action, or that foreign policy is an exception to this rule.

The preceding analysis has shown that the reason why foreign policy *ex ante* need not correspond to foreign policy *ex post* is the operation of adjustment processes. Every attempt at changing a foreign policy sets in motion a number of such processes; first, it generates external defensive adjustments. Assuming these defensive adjustments to be ineffectual, internal adjustment processes have to translate the change in one policy element into a change in the entire policy. Since on that level, too, one should expect negative adjustment processes to be at work, the outcome of every single foreign-policy move is far from being easily predictable. Secondly, the element of chance cannot be ignored either.

Foreign policy is thus undoubtedly a process of considerable complexity. Furthermore, it is also a large-scale process involving masses of men and resources. Given these conditions, the acquisition of information about the way foreign policy is performed and about the results it is producing becomes an important condition of political success. The ability correctly to appraise the progress of a foreign policy is important to policy-makers for two reasons: for the planning of future action, and for the justification and explanation of past and present action. In planning foreign policy, policy-makers need accurate information about progress to date and about the policies of other states. Secondly, the explanation and justification of policy, and consequently its criticism, present fewer difficulties if there is some agreed method of ascertaining the facts about a foreign policy. Historians who describe foreign policies and who attempt to estimate their effects may also need a framework for ordering their data.

For both these purposes, the concepts and generalizations devised here appear useful. Two approaches suggest themselves: one through power, and the other through aims.

As regards power, it is not inconceivable that an attempt should be made to record and to measure power-input and power-output. A yearly computation of power-input obtained by policy-makers could be compared with the record of power-output. The analysis of power-output discloses the nature and the amount of support upon which a government relies; an examination of power-output indicates the distribution of resources between various policies. With such information at their disposal, policy-makers could anticipate tendencies of power-output to exceed power-input, and vice versa. Partial methods of recording power-output are already available; the annual state budget is a yearly program of governmental action, and its implementation constitutes a record of its activities. But for foreign-policy purposes it presents only a part of the picture and it hardly ever reflects, *inter alia*, external power-input. While a completely reliable method of recording power-input and power-output remains to be developed, the field of inquiry is well enough defined, one may suggest, to warrant further study of this problem.

The concept of power-resources suggests ways of gauging the successes and the failures of a foreign policy. At any point of time, a state disposes of a definable stock of governmental and national assets and liabilities. This stock is subject to fluctuation, and a period in which power-resources have risen, and in which power-liabilities have fallen, may reasonably be said to have been a successful one. The gain or loss of territory has been an age-old criterion of success or failure in foreign policy. The task of further thought in this field would be to refine this common-sense insight and make it into a tool of systematic analysis.

With regard to the analysis of aims, the first step is, of course, to ascertain and to describe the input of demands confronting the policy-makers, and to compare it with the objectives of foreign-policy operations. Such a procedure might help in finding out the extent to which interests are in fact being reflected in objectives. These are, however, difficult problems, and they will remain signposts of further inquiry for students of foreign policy for a time to come. Public opinion analysis is a step forward on this road, but it covers too small a segment of the total interests to provide an answer to the problem.

The analysis of the changes in the composition of the community constitutes another approach to the problem of gauging the success of policy. We would assume here that a successful community tends to attract new members, and that dissatisfied groups tend to leave the community and refuse to cooperate with policy-makers. The number of states "lost to Communism" has been widely recognized as a contemporary criterion of American success. Increases or decreases in the number of enemies and in the size of the group of temporary collaborators are other significant criteria. The analysis of changes in the structure of the community does not appear to present insurmountable obstacles.

A balance sheet is a list of assets and liabilities as of a certain date and a summary of inputs and outputs over a certain period. A periodic drawing up of a balance sheet will disclose changes in assets and liabilities and in the rates of input and output. In business, the balance sheet is the chief instrument for judging a firm's success, and it is indispensable for the control of large-scale enterprises. It is here suggested that one might also prepare a balance sheet of a foreign policy. Such an inventory would show the state of the policy-makers' power-resources and liabilities and the composition of their community; it would also summarize the changes that have occurred, over a certain period, in the interests, objectives, power-input, and power-output of the policy. The metaphor of the balance sheet is, on occasions, used in the appraisal of foreign policy. Through foreign-policy analysis, the concept of a balance sheet of policy may be given a more precise meaning.